THE AUTHOR

Geoffrey Parrinder is Professor of the Comparative Study of Religions in the University of London. After ordination he spent twenty years teaching in West Africa and studying African religions, and became the founder member of the Department of Religious Studies in the University Collect of Ibadan, Nigeria. He has travelled widely in Africa, Sri Lanka, Burma, Iran, Israel, Jordan and Turkey and has lectured in Australia, America and India, and at Oxford. He is the author of many books on world religions which have been translated into eight languages.

Jesus in the Qur'ān

By the same author

West African Religion
Religion in Africa
Religion in an African City
African Mythology
The Story of Ketu
Witchcraft, European and African
The Christian Approach to the Animist
The Christian Debate
Comparative Religion
An Introduction to Asian Religions
The World's Living Religions
What World Religions Teach
A Dictionary of Non-Christian Religions
A Book of World Religions
Avatar and Incarnation
Upanishads, Gita and Bible
African Traditional Religion
The Bhagavad Gita: A Verse Translation
Worship in the World's Religions
The Indestructible Soul
The Wisdom of the Forest
Mysticism in the World's Religions

JESUS IN THE QUR'ĀN

GEOFFREY PARRINDER

OXFORD UNIVERSITY PRESS
New York
1977

First published in Great Britain in 1965
by Faber & Faber Ltd.

Reprinted in 1976 by Sheldon Press

First published in the United States in 1977
Oxford University Press
New York

Printed and bound in Great Britain

Contents

1

Introduction

THIS book has been written primarily for readers in the western world, the general public as well as students of theology and the comparative study of religions. But it is hoped that it may also be useful to some people in Asia and Africa who have asked for a modern and impartial study of the teaching of the Qur'ān about Jesus, which seems to be unobtainable in English or Arabic.

In the modern world the ease of communications and the growth of world languages enable the spoken or written word to be studied far away. A lecture given in London may be reported in Cairo, and a book written in New York may be read in Lahore or Tokyo. It is no longer possible to write or speak to a limited audience; all the world is listening. This means that when a westerner writes about another religion, say Islam, there is not just a Christian but a world audience. One cannot write about Islam in a vacuum, for Muslims will read. They may agree or disagree, and they are likely to be impressed or offended not only by what is said but by the way in which it is said, whether it is fair or prejudiced, sympathetic or antagonistic. As W. Cantwell Smith has said, one must try to write so that intelligent and honest Muslims will recognize what is said as accurate; in fact, 'no statement about a religion is valid unless it can be acknowledged by that religion's believers'.[1]

This is a study of religion, and it presupposes sympathy with

[1] *Islam in Modern History*, 1957, p. vi; and 'Comparative Religion: Whither – and Why?', in Eliade and Kitagawa, *The History of Religions*, 1959, pp. 42ff.

religious faith. The old idea that only an agnostic could write impartially is less popular now than in the last century, for it is realized that one who regards religion as superstition may well be biased and cannot hope to discover the inner spirit of religion or command the attention of believers. It is noteworthy that some of the most eminent modern writers on Islam in English, French and German are Christians who approach Islam as a kindred religion. But many academic scholars are interested chiefly in linguistic or historical matters, and questions of theology tend to get left aside for lack of interest or competence. When the theologian enters this field he must try to follow academic discipline, apply its standards in the examination of texts and teachings, yet bring out the meaning and importance of religion. This gives at least three classes of reader: academic, Christian and Muslim. It is indeed a world audience.[1]

The interest of this book is chiefly theological, and so questions of textual criticism, a subject peculiarly delicate for Muslims, have largely been left aside. Particularly, following the example of W. Montgomery Watt, 'in order to avoid deciding whether the Qur'ān is or is not the Word of God, I have refrained from using the expressions "God says" and "Muḥammad says" when referring to the Qur'ān, and have simply said "the Qur'ān says" '.[2]

The teaching of the Qur'ān is still little known in the Christian and western world. There are historical reasons of separation and enmity that led to misunderstanding and neglect, and these ought no longer to apply if we are to live as neighbours and friends in one world; but there are literary reasons too. The Qur'ān has rarely been well translated, and in translation it loses its poetic form and flavour. It is not an easy book to read, especially in its traditional arrangement with the longest chapters first. Yet there is a great deal of its material which parallels stories and teachings of the Bible, both Old and New Testaments. The texts that speak about Jesus are particularly important for Christians and Muslims, and it is hoped that it will be found useful to have these presented in a collected form. At the same time the context of the rest of the Qur'ān must not

[1] W. M. Watt, *Muhammad at Mecca*, 1953, p. x. [2] *ibid.*

be neglected. A selection cannot absolve the serious student from reading the whole book. It is not possible to understand Islam without studying all the Qur'ān, yet to study it brings its own reward and gives at least an impression of the religious fervour, originality and depth of this holy book. To read the scriptures of other people is most important in such highly literary religions, and as a Christian would recommend study of the Bible, and especially the Gospel, to his Muslim friends, so he may be urged to read and meditate on the Qur'ān.

In the following pages attempts are made to show what the Qur'ān says about Jesus, and to examine in what senses the Quranic teaching may be taken. Parallels are given to this teaching in the Gospel, where they occur. The many other teachings about Jesus found in the rest of the New Testament and the later church are not fully dealt with here, for that is another subject. But it may be remarked that Islam, when it left Arabia and entered into debate with Christians, came to see Christian teaching in dogmas which had been partly framed by Greek thought, both orthodox and heretical, and the Semitic thought of the Gospel was insufficiently known. Whether early Islam followed on the tradition of Jewish Christianity, as Harnack and others suggested, is a difficult question and beyond our present concern, though it is worthy of more research and fuller light may be shed on it by archaeological discovery.[1]

In the course of Islamic history various attitudes have been adopted towards Jesus. Some of these are based upon the Qur'ān, while others have been influenced by later commentary and the unhappy controversies that have made our religions appear as enemies rather than as allies. In modern times some leading Muslim writers, lay rather than professional theologians, have studied the Bible and written sympathetic accounts of Jesus as depicted there, while the authors have remained within the bounds of Islamic orthodoxy and personal faith. Certain extremists have gone on to criticize Jesus and his character, in a manner not only offensive to Christians but inconsistent with the teaching of both Qur'ān and Gospel.

[1] See on the Ebionites H. J. Schoeps, *Theologie und Geschichte des Juden-christentums*, 1949, pp. 334–42; and on the Qumran community and its possible influence on Islam, C. Rabin, *Qumran Studies*, 1957, pp. 116ff. and see below p. 100n.

In the following pages the Qur'ān itself is the principal object of study, with parallels in the Gospel where possible. Later Muslim commentary and interpretation are considered only slightly though they could not be ignored altogether. The chief authorities mentioned are: Ibn Isḥāq (d. A.D. 768; A.H. 151) whose Sīra, the Life of the Apostle, is the standard biography of Muḥammad as preserved by Ibn Hishām (d. 834); the collection of Ḥadīth or Traditions by Bukhārī (d. 870); the history and commentary of Ṭabarī (d. 923), and the commentaries of Zamakhsharī (d. 1144), Rāzī (d. 1209), and Baiḍāwī (d. 1282).[1] Baiḍāwī's commentary, summarizing earlier work, was regarded by orthodox Sunni Muslims almost as a holy book, it received more careful study than other commentaries, his discussions on a single chapter of the Qur'ān were expanded into whole books, his two volumes into eight, and many later works are based upon his. Some modern commentators and general writers have also been mentioned from time to time. But apart from characteristic and orthodox comments the attempt has been made to interpret the Qur'ān itself here, rather than later Islamic exposition, which is given only for illustration.

It is common nowadays to talk of 'return to the source texts', and there are movements of 'back to the Qur'ān' as there are of 'back to the Bible'. Biblical scholars recognize that it is hard to separate Scripture from Tradition, and in Islam the Qur'ān has been interpreted through the Ḥadīth and later traditions. Yet there is special value in going back as far as possible to the sacred texts. Christian and Muslim positions have been hardened over the centuries into formulas which cannot all claim the full authority of the original scriptures. Rather than enter into arguments over dogmatic statements which only lead to deadlock, it may be more profitable to prepare the ground for meeting and discussion by a return to the basic texts.[2]

A critical attitude to the traditions and commentaries has been expressed in modern studies of both Jesus and Muḥam-

[1] Most of these names are prefixed by *al-*, 'the', in Arabic, but non-Arabic-speaking Muslims do not use this definite article, it is tedious, and many Europeans follow them.

[2] See M. Hayek, *Le Christ de l'Islam*, 1959, p. 12; H. Michaud, *Jésus selon le Coran*, 1960, pp. 10f.; valuable books but rather biased, see pp. 166, 168f. below.

mad. Professor Isḥāq Ḥusaini says that the traditions 'do not, by any means, stand on the same footing as the Qur'ān . . . the authentic traditions are like a handful of grain in a heap of chaff'.[1] A Lebanese writer on pre-Islamic Arabia and the life of the Prophet, Muḥammad 'Izza Darwaza, takes the Qur'ān as the only source and sure witness and encourages a critical attitude to tradition. The great success of the life of the Prophet by Muḥammad Ḥussain Haykal in Egypt,[2] has been largely due to his use of 'scientific method', criticizing stories of tradition which shock modern views of the Prophet, and appealing to that large and growing Muslim public which has received a western-type education, is repelled by customary exposition, yet tries to practise its faith in the modern setting. And Dr Kamel Hussein has described as 'a fatuous innovation' the search for scientific inventions even in Quranic texts, and claims that modern Muslims must look for the fundamental principles to be applied to faith and life.[3]

The quotations from the Qur'ān in English given below are nearly all taken from Richard Bell's two volume *The Qur'ān translated*, published by Messrs T. & T. Clark of Edinburgh, to whom thanks are due for their permission of quotation. The verses given from the sūras are numbered first of all from Fluegel's edition, which is still generally used in the West, but as it does not correspond exactly to any Oriental recension the second reference in each verse is from the Cairo edition of 1923.

In some places A. J. Arberry's *The Koran Interpreted* has been followed. As in Professor Arberry's version, Allāh is always rendered here as God. It is increasingly recognized that for English-speaking people to insist on using only the word Allāh can be quite misleading. The thin English pronunciation makes it almost unintelligible to an Arabic-speaking Muslim. But also the sentimental associations of Allāh in the European's mind, and the notion that he is speaking about another God, are most deceptive. There are differences between the Muslim and the Christian apprehensions of God, but it would be fatal to any chance of understanding to doubt that one and the same God is

[1] *Christ in the Qur'ān and in Modern Arabic Literature*, Tokyo, 1960.
[2] Fifth edition, Cairo, 1960.
[3] See 'The Story of Adam', in *The Muslim World*, 1964, pp. 4ff.

the reality in both ('Our God and your God is One', see p. 165). Similarly 'Īsā is rendered as Jesus, Maryam as Mary, Injīl as Gospel, and Naṣārā as Christians, because no doubt this book will be read principally by those who are used to these forms.

Acknowledgements and grateful thanks are due to a number of friends. Professor Isḥāq Ḥusaini, Dr Kamel Hussein and the Rev. J. W. Bowker all read drafts of the manuscript and made helpful criticisms and suggestions. Lectures on some of the chapters were given at the University of Ibadan and under the Oxford University Extra-Mural Delegacy and gave rise to valuable discussion. Mr K. D. D. Henderson and the Spalding Trust helped to make possible a study visit to Cairo. Professor Ḥusaini and other members of the Center for Arabic Studies in the American University in Cairo were most kindly in providing references and interviews. Dr Murād Kāmil of Cairo University was valuable on Coptic and Ethiopic sources. Fr J. Jomier and other members of the Institut Dominicain d'Etudes Orientales du Caire helped with advice and hospitality. And I shall not forget the long discussions with Dr Kamel Hussein, author of *City of Wrong*, who took time off from a busy medical life to talk about problems of deep religious importance. The assurance that this book could be useful, and was not offensive to modern Muslims, encouraged the writer in final revisions and publication of a matter that had long been on his mind.

Although the interest of this book is religious and theological, it makes no claim to be either speculative or dogmatic theology. It has been said that the present time is for ploughing, not reaping, for making soundings, not plotting maps. Yet if the time is not ripe for major works of theological construction or reconstruction, the tools for this work need to be provided. These tools are known to specialists, but they should be made available to a much wider audience, for the encounter of the world religions is a major fact of our times and it demands a restatement of traditional theological expression. This restatement must take account of all the new knowledge available.

The present writer has often disagreed with some of the theological views of Dr Hendrik Kraemer, and he is glad therefore to support one of Dr Kraemer's latest pleas, in which he says, 'the "dialogue" with the non-Christian religions should not only be the concern of a few so-called experts, who are as Christians professional students of one or more of these religions. The period in which that could be the case has definitely passed. The time has now arrived when all theological thinkers have to include these new worlds of thought and apprehension in their sphere of interest. Not only for the *theoretical* reason of joining issue in philosophical and religious respect with thought- and life-systems, whose key concepts were for a long time mainly marginal in the cultural and religious world debate, but for *pastoral* reasons. This pastoral aspect deserves special mention, because the "ordinary" people turn in their perplexity in the first place not to the leading Christian thinkers, but to their ministers and pastors. In other words it demands a reorientation of the education of the ministry, a theology of religion and religions, which is more and something else than textbook or capsule knowledge of non-Christian religions.'[1]

Beyond the 'capsule' knowledge of Islam that one may pick up from a handbook on world religions, lie great matters such as the Islamic concept of God, the nature of man, freewill, immortality, and the place of Christ. Islam has been a closed world to Christians till modern times, and the teaching of the Qur'ān about Jesus is widely ignored. The present book seeks to present a compendium of Quranic teaching on this great subject. At the same time the Christian, and particularly the Biblical, teaching has been largely unknown in the past within 'the house of Islam'. Fuller study, not only of Biblical parallels to Quranic teaching, but also of other Biblical material which may legitimately be studied by a loyal Muslim, may bring a better knowledge of Jesus.

To Christians and to Muslims, to historians and to general readers, this book offers a new study of what the Qur'ān says concerning Jesus, together with similar sayings from the Gospel. It is hoped that this account of a matter of great common concern, by going back to the fundamental scriptures, will help to remove some misunderstandings and lead towards deeper appreciation of Muslim and Christian faith.

[1] *World Cultures and World Religions*, 1960, p. 365.

2

Jesus (ʻĪsā)

THE Qur'ān gives a greater number of honourable titles to Jesus than to any other figure of the past. He is a 'sign', a 'mercy', a 'witness' and an 'example'. He is called by his proper name Jesus, by the titles Messiah (Christ) and Son of Mary, and by the names Messenger, Prophet, Servant, Word and Spirit of God. The Qur'ān gives two accounts of the annunciation and birth of Jesus, and refers to his teachings and healings, and his death and exaltation. Three chapters or sūras of the Qur'ān are named after references to Jesus (3, 5 and 19); he is mentioned in fifteen sūras and ninety-three verses. Jesus is always spoken of in the Qur'ān with reverence; there is no breath of criticism, for he is the Christ of God.

The proper name of Jesus in the Qur'ān is ʻĪsā, which is used in the personal sense without explanation. The form of the name has given rise to considerable comment though there is general agreement that ʻĪsā came from the Syriac Yeshūʻ which derived it from the Hebrew Yeshua. Some western scholars have thought that the final vowel change was influenced by the analogy of Mūsā in Arabic for Moses (Mosheh), but only in five places is ʻĪsā mentioned along with Mūsā in the Qur'ān. Other western scholars have suggested that ʻĪsā was used by Arabian Jews about Jesus because of its similarity to Esau, and they are supposed to have said in scorn that the soul of Esau had been transferred to him.[1] But there is no evidence for this, and Jesus is never compared with Esau in the many volumes of the Tal-

[1] *Encyclopaedia of Islam*, 1913, article, ʻĪsā.

mud. Neither the Qur'ān nor later Islam have the contemptuous attitude to Jesus that some suggested derivations imply. If 'Īsā was a despised name then it would be impossible to understand why the Qur'ān used it for the venerated figure of the Messiah, and impossible also to understand why Jewish critics of Muhammad did not seize on this to discredit his revelations.

A modern theory has suggested that there might be a reference to 'Īsā in some pre-Islamic Arabian inscriptions, where the word *yt'* has been taken as a dialectical variant of *hys'* and thus as 'none other' than 'Īsā. But G. Ryckmans has strongly contested this view, saying that *yt'* cannot be identified with Jesus, and that outside these *yt'* texts there are no other mentions of Jesus except in two late and exclusively Christian Trinitarian inscriptions.[1]

The classical Muslim commentator al-Baiḍāwī dismissed fanciful efforts at providing an etymology for 'Īsā, such as one which would derive it from *'ayasun*, which means 'white with a shade of red'. He said that it was an arabized form of Ishu', probably meaning the Syriac Yeshū'.[2] Rāzī said that it was from Yasū' and this is what the Syrians say. It is possible that the pronunciation of the Syriac word was varied by Nestorian Christians in southern Syria and Arabia. It seems that there was a monastery in southern Syria which as early as A.D. 571 bore the name 'Īsānīya, 'of the followers of Jesus'.[3]

The European Christian form of the name Jesus is derived, of course, from the Greek Ἰησοῦς in the Gospel, which was a translation of the Hebrew Yeshua, a shortened form of Yehoshua (Joshua). The meaning of the name is 'God's salvation', or 'he whose salvation is Yahweh'.[4] The final 's' of the Greek and European words for Jesus is quite unsemitic. The old Syriac Yeshū' is preserved in the modern Arabic translation of the Gospel as Yasū'. It has been suggested that modern Christians in Arabic-speaking countries should use the name 'Īsā, as used

[1] G. Ryckmans, *Analecta Bollandia*, 1949, lxvii, pp. 62f.; *Les Religions Arabes préislamiques*, 1951, p. 48.

[2] Baiḍāwī's commentary was edited by H. O. Fleischer, 1848; a translation of sura 3 was made in 1894 by D. S. Margoliouth, in *Chrestomathia Baidawiana*.

[3] A. Jeffery, *The Foreign Vocabulary of the Qur'ān*, 1938, p. 219; A. Mingana, 'Syriac Influence on the Style of the Kur'ān', *Rylands Bulletin*, 1927.

[4] V. Taylor, *The Names of Jesus*, 1959, p. 5.

by all the Muslims around them. But the new translation of the Arabic New Testament, prepared by Professor 'Abd-al-Mālik in Cairo, retains Yasū' as the traditional and older form, and no Arab Christians appear to use the form 'Īsā.

The name 'Īsā occurs twenty-five times in the Qur'ān, and the use of other titles in conjunction with this or separately, such as Messiah and Son of Mary, means that Jesus is spoken of some thirty-five times. Most of these mentions are in some of those sūras of the Qur'ān which are traditionally ascribed to Medina, revealed after the Hijra in A.D. 622 (sūras 2, 3, 4, 5, 9, 33, 57, 61 all mention Jesus). Five of the sūras which name Jesus are placed at Mecca, revealed between 610 and 622 (6, 19, 23, 42, 43; and a reference in 21 also). Of the latter, sūra 19 is particularly important because it contains one of the two accounts of the birth of Jesus. Bell and other western commentators see Medinan traits in this sūra, but they admit that there seems to be a Meccan basis for it. The Medinan sūras are probably directed towards Christians more than are the Meccan, and so Jesus is mentioned more often. But the repetition of the birth story (sūras 3 and 19) may be on account of the different audiences of Mecca and Medina. Many other Quranic stories occur several times; for example, those of Moses, Thamūd, Iblīs, Solomon.

All the mentions of Jesus in the Qur'ān will be discussed in the course of this book. Here they are listed for convenience of reference, in the traditional order of the sūras:

2,81/87: 'We gave Jesus, son of Mary, the Evidences and aided him by the Holy Spirit.'

2,130/136: 'What has been given to Moses and Jesus and the prophets.'

2,254/253: 'We gave Jesus, son of Mary, the Evidences and supported him by the Holy Spirit.'

3,40/45: 'God giveth thee tidings of a word from himself whose name is the Messiah, Jesus, son of Mary.'

3,45/52: 'Jesus perceived unbelief on their part.'

3,48/55: 'God said: "O Jesus, I am going to bring thy term to an end and raise thee to myself".'

3,52/59: 'Jesus in God's eyes is in the same position as Adam.'

3,78/84: 'What was given to Moses and Jesus and the prophets.'

4,156/157: 'For their saying: "We killed the Messiah, Jesus, son of Mary, the messenger of God".'

4,161/163: 'We made suggestions to ... the Patriarchs, to Jesus,' etc.

4,169/171: 'The Messiah, Jesus, son of Mary, is only the messenger of God, and his word which he cast upon Mary, and a spirit from him.'

4,170/172: 'The Messiah will not disdain to be a servant of God.'

5,19/17: 'They have disbelieved who say that God is the Messiah, the son of Mary ... if he wisheth to destroy the Messiah, son of Mary, and his mother.'

5,50/46: 'In their footsteps we caused Jesus, son of Mary, to follow.'

5,76/72: 'They have disbelieved who say: "God is the Messiah, son of Mary".'

5,79/75: 'The Messiah, son of Mary, is nothing but a messenger.'

5,82/78: 'Those ... who have disbelieved were cursed by the tongue of David and Jesus, son of Mary.'

5,109/110: 'O Jesus, son of Mary, remember my goodness to thee.'

5,112: 'The apostles said: "O Jesus, son of Mary, is thy Lord able to send down to us a table from heaven?" '

5,114: 'Jesus, son of Mary, said: "O God our Lord".'

5,116: 'God said: "O Jesus, son of Mary, was it thou who didst say to the people",' etc.

6,85: 'Zachariah and John and Jesus and Elijah.'

9,30: 'Christians say that the Messiah is the son of God.'

9,31: 'Monks as Lords apart from God, as well as the Messiah, son of Mary.'

19,35/34: 'That is Jesus, son of Mary, a statement of the truth.'

21,91: 'We ... made her and her son a sign to the worlds.'

23,52/50: 'We appointed the Son of Mary and his mother to be a sign.'

33,7: 'Noah, and Abraham, and Moses and Jesus, son of Mary.'

42,11/13: 'What we laid as a charge upon Abraham and Moses and Jesus.'

43,57: 'When the Son of Mary is used as a parable.'

43,63: 'When Jesus came with the Evidences.'

57,27: 'In their footsteps we caused our messengers to follow, and we caused Jesus, son of Mary, to follow, and we gave him the Gospel.'

61,6: 'Jesus, son of Mary, said: "O children of Israel, I am God's messenger to you".'

61,14: 'Jesus, son of Mary, said to the apostles: "Who are my helpers towards God?" '

This bare enumeration of the references to Jesus by one of his names in the Qur'ān does not show, of course, the difference between passing allusions and longer narratives in which Jesus is the central figure. It is hoped that this will become clearer in the ensuing chapters. But the list may be useful for reference, and having been given here it will not be necessary to give separately all the references to some of the other names, for example, Son of Mary.

This list may give some indication of different lines of Quranic teaching about Jesus. But if one verse or another appears surprising it should be studied in its context. All the difficult verses will be discussed later in this book. The problems of the birth of Jesus, the crucifixion and the Trinity will all be considered.

The Qur'ān honours Jesus, and following its teaching Islam has done the same. There are many later stories of his poverty, charity and benevolence. The mutual misunderstandings of Christians and Muslims have led at times to depreciation of Jesus or the Gospel, but Muslims generally have distinguished between Jesus and his followers. Still today when his name is mentioned the pious Muslim says: 'Īsā, on whom be peace.' This may be derived from the Qur'ān, which attributes these words to Jesus: 'Peace is upon me the day of my birth, and the day of my death, and the day of my being raised up alive.' (sūra 19,34/33) But the phrase is used of other prophets too.

In Christianity the name Jesus has always been taken as his personal name. In the Gospel it is said that the angel told

Joseph and Mary, 'thou shalt call his name Jesus; for it is he that shall save his people from their sins'. (Matt. 1,21; Lk. 1,31) In the Gospels the name Jesus occurs hundreds of times, and only occasionally with the addition of 'the Nazarene' or 'of Nazareth'. The Qur'ān does not mention the town of Nazareth, though Christians are regularly termed Naṣārā. The double name 'Jesus Christ' is very rare in the Gospel; there are some four certain examples. 'Christ Jesus' and 'Lord Jesus' never occur here. This shows the primitive and narrative usage of the Gospel.

By contrast the Epistles use the names Jesus Christ, Christ Jesus, and the Lord Jesus Christ very frequently. Paul, however, uses the name Jesus alone eighteen times, and there are nine instances in the rather Jewish and anonymous epistle to the Hebrews. In the narrative book of Acts the name Jesus is found more than any other, and also it receives qualifying terms such as Jesus 'of Nazareth', 'this same Jesus', 'his servant Jesus', and 'thy holy servant Jesus'.[1]

The name Jesus was common in the first century. Bar-Jesus and Jesus Justus are mentioned in the New Testament, and the Jewish historian Josephus refers to about twenty people with this name. But after the first century both Christians and Jews avoided giving this name to their children. In later Christianity the titles Jesus Christ or Christ alone seem to have been more common than Jesus by itself; though litanies of the Holy Name and the Jesus-prayer of the eastern churches have stressed this name. Since the beginning of the modern critical study of the Bible the name Jesus has perhaps come to be used more often by Christians, to stress the humanity of Jesus and sometimes in an effort to distinguish between 'the Jesus of history' and 'the Christ of faith'. How legitimate this is has often been debated, and to pursue it is beyond our purpose here which is not dogmatic but expository, to consider the Quranic teaching and the Biblical only so far as it is parallel to the Qur'ān.

[1] V. Taylor, *The Names of Jesus*, pp. 5f.

3

Son of Mary (Ibn Maryam)

It will have been noticed in the list of references to Jesus in the Qur'ān, given in the last chapter, that one of the commonest titles for him is Son of Mary (Ibn Maryam). This metronymic occurs twenty-three times in the Qur'ān, sixteen times as Jesus, son of Mary, and seven times as Son of Mary alone or with some other title. This is surprising, since Son of Mary occurs only once in the Bible.

The story of the birth of Jesus from Mary is given in some detail twice in the Qur'ān. Indeed the angels announce to Mary the coming of a word from God 'whose name is the Messiah, Jesus, son of Mary'. (3,40/45) Then again, 'the Son of Mary and his mother' are said to have been appointed as a sign, for he gave the Evidences or proofs of God. (2,81/87; 2,254/253; 23,52/50; 43,63) 'The Son of Mary is used as a parable' against the polytheists, for he came with Wisdom, to make differences clear and to show piety towards God. (43,57–63)

The title Son of Mary is so remarkable that some time must be spent discussing it. A modern commentator says that 'the epithet Ibn Maryam (Son of Mary) is added to show that he was a mortal like other prophets of God'.[1] This appears to assume too much. Baiḍāwī said that while Ibn Maryam is treated as a name, an epithet which distinguishes in the same way that a name does, yet it was used by the angels in speaking to Mary to call attention to the fact that Jesus would be born

[1] M. 'Alī, Translation and Commentary on *The Holy Qur'ān*, 4th edn., Lahore 1951, p. 40n.

without a father, since children are called after the father, and not the mother, except where the father is not known. This also may be reading too much into this title.

The Qur'ān does not mention Joseph who, according to two Gospels, was the father or foster-father of Jesus. (Matt. 1,19f.; but see Luke 2,33, 'his father') But the Qur'ān rebuts Jewish suggestions that there was any stigma in the birth of Jesus; 'his mother was a faithful woman', 'she guarded her chastity', 'one of the devout', God chose her 'above the women of the worlds'. (5,79/75; 21,91; 66,12; 3,37/42)

In using the title Son of Mary there is no hint in the Qur'ān of any criticism of either Mary or Jesus; it is used as a name like 'Īsā. While it is the normal thing in the Semitic world for a man to be called after his father, yet there are instances of men being called after their mothers. The poets Ibn 'Ā'isha and Ibn Mayyāda were thus known. One of 'Alī's sons was called after his mother, perhaps to distinguish him from two brothers with similar first names. Muḥammad himself was sometimes called Ibn Abī Kabsha, perhaps because of the connexion of one of his ancestors with such a name at Medina. Muḥammad's opponent, Abū Jahl, was sometimes called after his mother, and this may show that there were strong matrilineal ideas in certain Arabian families still surviving in the sixth century.[1] No Arab therefore would regard the name Son of Mary as an insult. To call Jesus after his mother may mean that his mother had become so well known, 'above the women of the worlds', that this was the most appropriate title.

In Christianity the title 'Son of Mary' has been exceedingly rare and it is worth considering this at some length. The only instance in the whole of the New Testament is in Mark 6,3: 'Is not this the carpenter, the son of Mary?' It seems surprising that the title should come in Mark, who has no mention of a virgin birth of Jesus, but it may be noted that Joseph is not mentioned in Mark. Matthew and Luke, who do have infancy stories, vary this question. Matthew 13,55 gives: 'Is not this the carpenter's son? Is not his mother called Mary?' Apparently

[1] W. M. Watt, *Muhammad at Medina,* 1956, p. 374. In some Arabian tribes sons still bear their mothers' names.

Matthew did not like to call Jesus the carpenter, but he retains the mention of Mary alone. Luke 4,22 says bluntly, 'Is not this Joseph's son?'

Modern commentators have been worried about Mark's verse, for it is agreed that Mark's Gospel was written first and was used by the other evangelists. All the great uncial manuscripts, and many minuscules, support our reading of Mark; though some minuscules and the commentator Origen give the reading, 'the son of the carpenter and of Mary'. Comparing this with Matthew a standard modern writer, Vincent Taylor, says that one would have thought that Matthew, with his story of the virgin birth, would have preferred to speak of Jesus as Son of Mary. This was 'a phrase congenial to his mind, and it is not easy to think that he would have used instead the words "the son of the carpenter" unless they already stood in Mark'. So Taylor concludes that Mark must originally have written 'the carpenter's son', and that an early scribe replaced this by 'the carpenter' and added 'the son of Mary'.[1] The reasoning is ingenious, but the evidence is weak. It might more simply be said that Mark used Son of Mary because Joseph was unknown to him, or dead, and Mary more prominent in the early church.

Another commentator, R. H. Lightfoot, suggests that there were insulting implications in the title used of Jesus by his critics at Nazareth, and only preserved in Mark. 'The Son of Mary . . . as used by the people of Jesus' acquaintance, it is most unnatural, and was presumably meant to be derogatory in the highest degree. No man in the East, whether his father were living or not, would be known familiarly by reference to his mother . . . except presumably with purpose to insult.'[2]

This seems rather strong, in view of Arabic instances we have noted of men called after their mothers. E. F. F. Bishop, who knows eastern countries well, puts another viewpoint. 'It is comparatively rare for a man to be known by his "metronymic". Perhaps Matthew realized this fact and thought the description

[1] V. Taylor, *The Gospel according to St Mark*, 1952, p. 300. I am indebted to Professor D. E. Nineham for references on this verse.

[2] *History and Interpretation of the Gospels*, 1935, p. 187.

a mistake. But other instances can be found. . . . It does seem unlikely that this Markan reference could be to the Virgin Birth. But it is not at all impossible that because of the name our Lord was making for himself, his Mother, presumably a widow by this time, would naturally become known. If the allusion is a matter of opprobrium, this is its only occurrence in the New Testament, but in the course of history the phrase has become well known throughout the Islamic world. The Qur'ān repeatedly speaks of him as "Jesus the Messiah, son of Mary". Here it is honorific as it must have been in the Ethiopic church which gave it to the Muslims.'[1]

This rather mysterious last phrase refers back to an article this writer had published some years earlier in which he said that the use of the title Son of Mary 'coincided with the return of the second group of emigrants, who would naturally tell . . . of the Abyssinian regard for the Virgin . . . as of the Virgin Birth. . . . A combination of circumstances therefore would seem to have been behind this free use of the phrase, the actual source for its use in early Islam coming most probably from Abyssinia.'[2]

The evidence for this is thin. The second party of returning Muslim migrants from Abyssinia appears to have arrived in Medina well after the Hijra, about A.H. 7; though some Western historians think there was only one migration to Abyssinia. However a first party is said to have returned to Mecca before the Hijra and to have taken part in the battle of Badr.[3] The title Son of Mary comes in some of the Meccan sūras, as well as the Medinan, so its use could hardly have depended on a second party of migrants.

But did the Abyssinian church use this title Son of Mary? It seems unlikely. The Abyssinians were divided in their interpretation of the nature of Jesus, some maintaining that he was human only, though divinity was later infused into him. The normal Monophysite view, which dominates the Ethiopian and Coptic churches, allows Jesus even less humanity. It does not

[1] *Jesus of Palestine*, 1955, pp. 61f.

[2] Article, 'The Son of Mary', in *The Moslem World*, July 1934; I am grateful to the Rev. E. F. F. Bishop for correspondence on this point.

[3] See lists in *Muhammad at Mecca*, pp. 110f., 183ff.

appear from the Christological controversies that the title Son of Mary was used in story or liturgy in Abyssinia. If research finds this it will be significant, but Dr Murād Kāmil declares that it is impossible.

Ethiopic, the ancient language of Abyssinia, is the most closely related to Arabic of all Semitic languages, and these two are grouped together as South Semitic in distinction from the North Semitic group. Yet despite the close relationships that existed between the Ḥijāz and Abyssinia in the time of Muḥammad, very few religious terms seem to have come into Arabic from Ethiopic. Injīl for Gospel, and Ḥawārīyūn for Apostles, are generally taken to be of Ethiopic origin but little else. The Christian communities in South Arabia were mixed, some being Nestorians, others Jacobites or Syrians, and others Monophysites like the Abyssinians. Muḥammad himself had debates with South Arabian Christians, but his chief contacts are more likely to have been with the north, and he had travelled to Syria where there were many Christians. Most of the foreign religious terms found in the Qur'ān seem to be derived from or through Syriac, and it has been estimated that Ethiopic linguistic influences are only about five per cent, whereas the Syriac are over seventy per cent.[1]

The use of the title Son of Mary, found only once in the Bible, was not taken up by the early church generally. A search in the orthodox Christian literature of the centuries after the Bible was written has found no trace of this title, though it is possible that it was used occasionally or obscurely. Even apocryphal and heretical works rarely use it. The 'apocrypha' after the New Testament are writings whose origin was unknown or which were not included in the canon of orthodox scripture. The so-called apocryphal 'Gospels' are legendary or mostly Gnostic speculations, and deal with stories of the infancy and youth of Jesus which are not mentioned in the canonical scriptures. Since 1946 new apocrypha have been found near Nag-Hammadi, north of Luxor in Egypt, and these contain Gnostic Gospels, Acts and Apocalypses. From what has so far

[1] A. Jeffery, *The Foreign Vocabulary of the Qur'ān*, pp. 12–20, 71; A. Mingana, *Syriac Influence on the Style of the Kur'ān*, pp. 6, 22.

appeared these are fanciful productions and secondary to the true Gospels.[1]

In the standard collection of New Testament apocrypha by M. R. James the title Son of Mary does occur, but significantly enough only in the Arabic and Syriac Gospels of the Infancy. It may have been used elsewhere, and if that is shown it will be important. But the Syriac and Arabic usage is further evidence for the belief that Syrian Christian contacts were the closest for early Islam.

Our chief knowledge of the Arabic Gospel of the Infancy of Jesùs depends upon a version edited in 1697 by the German orientalist Sike, and based upon an original which has since been lost. There are unpublished texts of this apocryphal writing at Florence and Rome. The date of this Gospel is uncertain, though in the French edition by P. Peeters the editor says that the anecdotes in the book 'must have been current fairly early among Arab Christians because they passed into the Qur'ān'. This statement may be challenged because while some of these infancy stories can be paralleled in the Qur'ān in part, the very ones that use the title Son of Mary have no counterpart in the Qur'ān. The Arabic Infancy Gospel may itself be post-Islamic and influenced by Muslim usage, though behind it is the older Syriac.

In the Arabic Infancy Gospel the title Son of Mary occurs five times. Because of the inaccessibility of this document it is worth quoting. In chapter 18 a leprous girl washes herself with bath water that had been used for the baby Jesus, is cleansed and says: 'I was leprous and I have been purified by . . . Jesus, the son of Lady Mary.' Later a young girl is possessed by a demon, but when she is protected by a swaddling cloth belonging to the infant Jesus, the demon is driven out by flames coming from it and cries out, 'What do you want of me, Jesus, son of Mary? Where can I escape from you?' And he flees away.

[1] The most convenient one-volume collection of apocrypha is still that by M. R. James, *The Apocryphal New Testament*, 1924. But see also: H. J. Bardsley, *Reconstructions of Early Christian Documents* I, 1935; H. J. Schonfield, *Readings from the Apocryphal Gospels*, 1940; B. Altaner, *Patrology*, E.T. 1960; J. Doresse, *The Secret Books of the Egyptian Gnostics*, E.T. 1960; R. M. Grant and D. N. Freedman, *The Secret Sayings of Jesus*, 1960.

Later the child Jesus goes into a dyer's shop and throws all the clothes into one indigo vat. The dyer protests, 'What have you done to me, son of Mary?' Jesus then changes the clothes into robes of fine colours. Though not in the Qur'ān this story is found in later Muslim legend. Finally the child Jesus changes children into sheep and their mothers exclaim, 'O our Lord, Jesus, son of Mary! You are indeed the shepherd of Israel.' The mothers then tell their children to do whatever the Son of Mary says.[1]

In the Syriac Infancy Gospel the title Son of Mary occurs fifteen times, chiefly in childhood stories with Mary, but also in versions of the Biblical stories of Cana, Nain, Pilate and the empty tomb. In the parallel to the Arabic story of the girl possessed by a demon the Syriac version uses the more evangelical sentence, 'What have I to do with thee, O Jesus the Nazarene?' (See Mark 1,24.) But perhaps most significant in the Syriac version is an account of a debate between Christians and Jews in which the latter say, 'This man of whom ye speak who hath called himself the Son of God is the Son of Mary . . . Whence can ye show us that the Son of Mary is the Christ?'[2] This could suggest that Son of Mary may have been used by Jews in debate, though there was no reason why Christians should not use it also, and clearly some Syrian and Arab Christians did so. It may be noted that the Qur'ān not only calls Jesus Son of Mary but also Christ (Messiah) without question. Its chief objection is to the term Son of God, and perhaps Son of Mary is used in preference because Jesus was undoubtedly the Son of Mary.

As history these Infancy Gospels are worthless, and undeserving of the title Gospel; they are fanciful and vulgar legends, with no parallel in either Qur'ān or canonical Gospels. Their interest lies in the fact that the title Son of Mary was used in some Christian circles, in a fully honorific manner, and this shows the links between Syria and Arabia. Although the dates cannot be fixed precisely it is clear that the Arabic version depends upon the Syriac. Peeters, approved by Altaner, con-

[1] P. Peeters, *Evangiles apocryphes*, 1914, ii, pp. 20, 40ff.

[2] E. A. W. Budge, *The History of the Blessed Virgin Mary*, from the Syriac, 1899, pp. 76ff.

siders that the Syriac source of this and other apocrypha originated before A.D. 400.

In later and modern Christianity the title Son of Mary has not been common, though there is no doctrinal objection to it. Vincent Taylor says that 'remarkable is the way in which this name came to establish itself in the language of Christian devotion'.[1] In fact, it seems to be comparatively rare. In the Litany of the Most Holy Name of Jesus there is the title, among many others, 'Jesus, child of the Virgin Mary'. But other litanies are more concerned to stress Mary's side as Mother of Christ and God-bearer (Dei Genetrix, the phrase disputed by Nestorius, of which more later). There is a modern hymn with the refrain, 'Jesu, son of Mary, hear'. Altered in some Victorian hymn books to 'Jesu, son of David', the proper title 'Son of Mary' has now been generally restored.

In later Islam the title Son of Mary has been common. In Zamakhsharī's commentary on the Qur'ān 'the sermons of Jesus, son of Mary' are quoted. And Ibn 'Abbās tells the story of the call of the disciples when they were fishermen; they asked Jesus who he was, and he replied, 'I am Jesus, son of Mary, God's servant and apostle.' There are many such stories.[2]

This excursus has tried to show that while the title Son of Mary occurs only once in the Bible, and appears in Syriac and Arabic apocrypha, it was popularized by Islam through the Qur'ān. It is acceptable to both Muslims and Christians, for it is always used in their writings as an honourable name.

[1] *The Names of Jesus*, p. 11.

[2] See J. Robson, *Christ in Islam*, 1929, pp. 35ff.; A Jeffery, *A Reader on Islam*, 1962, pp. 574f.

4

Names of Jesus

(a) The Messiah (Al-Masīḥ)

JESUS receives the title Messiah (Christ) eleven times in the Qur'ān, all in Medinan sūras (3,40/45; 4,156/157; 4,169/171; 4,170/172; 5,19/17 twice; 5,76/72 twice; 5,79/75; 9,30; 9,31). Sura 3,40/45 relating the Annunciation of the birth of Jesus says: 'His name shall be the Messiah, Jesus, son of Mary' (or 'whose name is Messiah', Arberry's translation). The title is used in a personal way like Jesus, as in 5,76/72: 'The Messiah said, "O children of Israel, serve God".'

While no explanation is offered of the title Messiah, and it is applied to Jesus at all periods of his life from birth to exaltation, yet it appears to have a particular sense. 'O People of the Book, do not go beyond bounds in your religion, and do not say about God anything but the truth. The Messiah, Jesus, son of Mary, is only the messenger of God.' (4,169/171) And again, 'the Messiah, son of Mary, is nothing but a messenger, before whose time the messengers have passed away' (or, 'was only a messenger'). (5,79/75) On the negative side this is a defence of the unity and transcendence of God. On the positive side it places the Messiah in the succession of messengers and prophets of the past, in fact as succeeding to Old Testament prophecy.

The Messiah is also spoken of with angels. 'The Messiah will not disdain to be a servant of God, nor will the angels who stand in his presence.' (4,170/172) And in his defence against the Jews it is stated: 'for their saying, "We killed the Messiah, Jesus, son of Mary, the messenger of God", though they did not kill him and did not crucify him'. (4,156/157) This vital passage will be considered later, in connexion with the death of Jesus, but it seems to be a declaration that the Jews alone could not kill the Messiah of God and thwart the divine plans.

Two verses of the Qur'ān contain the difficult phrase, 'they have disbelieved who say that God is the Messiah, son of Mary'. (5,19/17; 5,76/72) This will be discussed later, on the Trinity; but as stated it could refer to a Christian heresy, the error of Patripassianism, that is, that God the Father suffered on the cross.

While there is no Quranic etymological explanation of the word Masīḥ, it was not difficult for the commentators to find a number of meanings. The origin is of course ultimately Hebrew, through the Syriac, but it seems to have been well known in north and south Arabia in pre-Islamic times. The Hebrew *mashiaḥ* was used of kings and patriarchs, and especially of the coming Deliverer. This was translated in the Septuagint Greek version of the Old Testament as 'Christos'.

Firozābādī in his Arabic dictionary said that there were over fifty explanations of Masīḥ. Zamakhsharī and Baiḍāwī admitted that it was a foreign word, and the latter commented that Masīḥ was the surname of Jesus, a title of honour like al-Ṣiddīq, the 'truthful', a surname of Abū Bakr the first caliph. That the Hebrew original was used of the 'anointed' kings of Israel and then for the coming Christ, was known to Muslim commentators and they tried to show how Jesus was anointed in this sense. The Qur'ān said that Jesus had been 'blessed' by God (19,32/31) and so anointed with honour; he had been protected from Satan from birth (3,31/36), he had been blessed by his special birth and compared only with Adam the father of mankind. (3,52/59; 7,171/172) Some found the etymology of the word in a root *msh*, 'to touch'. So Jesus was one whose touch purified from faults, being himself provided with the protection of the divine blessing and anointed with the blessed oil with which former prophets were anointed. Jesus himself anointed the needy, healing the blind, laying hands on the sick, and using oil for blessing. This is suggested in the Qur'ān (3,43/49), and it is explicit in the Gospel. (Mark 6,13; James 5,14) The

Qur'ān twice says that Jesus was 'supported [or 'confirmed'] by the Holy Spirit' (2,254/253; 5,109/110), and in the Gospel the coming of the Holy Spirit upon Jesus at his baptism was his anointing and suggests the beginning of his consciousness of being the Messiah (Mark 1,11 referring back to well-known Messianic prophecies).

Rāzī and others suggested a derivation of Masīh from a verb meaning 'to travel', for Jesus was said to have travelled much or gone on pilgrimage. For later Muslims Jesus became the model of pilgrims and the example of mystics. 'Take Jesus as your pattern,' said the theologian-mystic al-Ghazālī. Aḥmadīs have applied this idea of the wandering Jesus to their belief that he travelled eastwards as far as Kashmir.[1]

Christian use of the title Messiah is complex. Critical scholars consider that in the Gospel Jesus rarely or never applied this title to himself; and it may be noted that the Qur'ān never puts it in his mouth either. It does not occur used directly of Jesus for himself in Mark, or in Q (the 'source', *quelle*, of sayings of Jesus common to Matthew and Luke). It is commoner, significantly, in the birth stories used about but not by Jesus. 'We are entitled to conclude, on the basis of the evidence, that Jesus did not speak of himself as "the Christ". This silence does not mean that he did not believe himself to be the Messiah . . . His unwillingness to use the title must mean that he repudiated the current nationalistic expectations associated with it, feeling the need of a name more suited to express the nature of his mission for men.' Perhaps Jesus expressed his own views under the more enigmatic title Son of Man.[2]

The early church, however, had no hesitation in claiming Jesus as Messiah, despite the crucifixion; he had been proved to be such by the resurrection. Peter is said to have told the Jews at Pentecost, 'God hath made him both Lord and Christ, this Jesus whom you crucified'. (Acts 2,36) Cullmann remarks that after the peculiar reserve exercised by Jesus in the use of this name it was 'really ironical that the title Messiah . . . should have been deliberately, permanently connected with the name Jesus. The designation even gave the new faith its name.' The

[1] M. 'Alī, *Holy Qur'ān*, p. 142.

[2] *The Names of Jesus*, p. 20.

early Jewish church 'applied to Jesus certain specific ideas taken from the Jewish messianic expectation. It emphasized that Jesus appeared on earth as the Son of David, that he exercises kingship over his church, and that he will appear on earth as Messiah at the end.'[1]

But Christianity expanded largely outside the Jewish world and the early ideas tended to be replaced. 'In the Gentile world the term "Messiah" was meaningless, unless explained, and when explained was felt to be strange. Further the term was patently inadequate . . . The name "Christ" could only survive by becoming a personal designation, charged with deep religious meaning.' Earlier Messianic views gave way to other Christological views as soon as Christ was used as a proper name.[2]

The transformation that had come in Christian usage over the Jewish term Messiah, and the religious connotation of the name Christ, is perhaps reflected in the Quranic verse, 'the Christians . . . take their scholars and monks as lords apart from God, as well as the Messiah, son of Mary'. (9,31) There may be a reference here to the cult of saints, which affected parts of later Islam as well as Christianity, though Christian theologians have tried to distinguish between reverence given to saints and the worship which alone is due to God.

Later Islam often spoke of 'the Messiah, Peace be upon him!' But the interpretation of the Messianic concept in a special kingly or historical manner seems hardly to have been discussed yet in the Muslim world. In an Egyptian book, *The Genius of Christ*, the Messianic concept has been discussed in Hebrew history but not pursued for an interpretation of later Christian teaching.[3] But a modern Persian writer, in a study of Jesus, says, 'to be Messiah is not the lot of every ordinary man; only he who served humanity more than others and gave himself for it, could attain to this dignity'.[4]

In popular Muslim usage the name of Messiah is prefixed with the word al-Sayyid, 'the lord', which is a mark of honour.

[1] *The Christology of the New Testament*, E.T. 1959, pp. 113, 136.
[2] *Names*, pp. 22f.; Cullmann, p. 136.
[3] by 'Abbās Maḥmūd al 'Aqqād, 1952.
[4] *Seven Faces*, by Shīn Parto, Teheran.

The title al-Sayyid is used particularly for Muḥammad and his descendants, but also for some other great people. In *City of Wrong*, a study of Jerusalem on Good Friday from an orthodox Muslim point of view, the title 'the Lord Christ' is regularly used.[1] While appropriate to Muslims, this term has of course been invested by Christians with special devotional significance.

(b) Servant (*'abd*)

Jesus is called Servant of God in the Qur'ān, and while this title may not appear remarkable yet in the Bible it has associations with the Messiah.

The Quranic references are:

4,170/172: 'The Messiah will not disdain to be a servant of God, nor will the angels who stand in his presence' (lit. 'Who are brought near', or 'who are stationed near him').

19,31/30: 'Jesus said: "Lo I am the servant of God; he hath bestowed on me the Book and hath made me a prophet."'

43,57–61: 'When the Son of Mary is used as a parable . . . he is only a servant on whom we have bestowed favour, and have appointed him to be a parable for the Childen of Israel . . . Verily it [or 'he'] is knowledge [or 'a sign'] for the Hour.'

A canonical variation in the last sentence allowed commentators to regard the second coming of Jesus as a sign of the Last Day. (See page 124 later.)

The word *'abd* means a servant, and the Encyclopaedia of Islam says that it is 'best rendered theologically by our "creature"; man, for Islām, is the property of Allāh and not simply his servant'.[2] This does not mean that *'abd* is always interchangeable with the word 'man'. For in 4,170/172, quoted above, the angels too are called servants. They are messengers of God, and his creatures, but they are superhuman. But *'abd* has a deeper sense in its association with submission and worship. Jeffery says that 'if its primitive meaning is to worship, then the word retains this primitive meaning in Arabic and all the others are derived meanings'. It is possible that it came from words meaning making and serving, and so it was used of

[1] by M. Kamel Hussein, tr. K. Cragg, 1959, p. 215.

[2] art. 'Īsā.

divine service. In the sense of worship and worshipper 'it came to the Arabs from their neighbours in pre-Islamic times'.[1]

To be an *'abd* does not imply the harsh bondage that is associated with slavery, but complete surrender to or worship of God; the relationship is religious rather than social. This is clear in the use of *'abd* in Muslim personal and family names. The Beautiful Names of God (al-Asmā' al-Ḥusnā) are used in construct form with the word *'abd*. Only rarely is a name found like 'Abd al-Khalīfa, 'servant of the caliph', but the strict Muslim will not call a person the *'abd* of any man but only of God. So one of the Ninety-nine names, or one of the many hundreds of other attribute names of God, is used: 'servant of God', 'servant of the King', 'servant of the Merciful' ('abd Allāh, 'abd al-Mālik, 'abd al-Raḥmān). The names of God enter as largely into naming as into Muslim praying, and the *'abd* indicates one who is fully surrendered to the worship of God.

It is said that the title *'abd* shows the humanity of Jesus as a servant. This is not surprising, for Christianity as well as Islam teaches the humanity of Jesus, or at least it does so in its orthodox and Biblical forms. On sura 43,59 a modern commentator remarks that Jesus 'was a righteous servant of Allāh on whom he had bestowed favours. Not only was he the recipient of favours, but he was also an example of virtue for the Israelites'.[2] But it is possible that there is in addition here an echo of the Gospel saying at the baptism of Jesus, 'in thee I am well pleased'. This verse is referred back to the Old Testament prophecy, 'My servant . . . in whom my soul delighteth'. (Mark 1,11; Isaiah 42,1)

The Arabic *'abd* is related to the Hebrew *'ebed*. The figure of the Servant of God (*'ebed Yahweh*) is of great importance in the book of Isaiah, especially in Isaiah 42,1: 'Behold my servant whom I uphold; my chosen, in whom my soul delighteth: I have put my spirit upon him.' (see sūras 2,254/253; 5,109/110) 'supported him by the Holy Spirit'. Again, in Isaiah 52,13–53,12 there is the famous Servant Song, 'Behold my servant shall deal wisely', etc. Whether the Servant of God here was meant to indicate a suffering prophet, or the people of Israel

[1] *Foreign Vocabulary of the Qur'ān*, p. 209.

[2] M. 'Alī, *Holy Qur'ān*, p. 936.

in their exile, or to suggest the Messiah, has long been disputed. But Christians soon identified the Messiah with the Suffering Servant. They would have agreed with the Qur'ān that the Messiah would not disdain to be the servant of God, for this was not a lowly but a great title, the *'ebed Yahweh.*

The title Servant is not put directly into the mouth of Jesus in the Gospels, but there are references to the above quotations from Isaiah. The words at the baptism have been mentioned. Later in predictions of the passion it is said that 'the Son of Man must suffer', and 'he was reckoned with the transgressors', and 'himself took our infirmities and bore our diseases'. (Mk. 8,31f.; Lk. 22,37; Matt. 8,17) The words of Jesus on the Son of Man giving his life 'a ransom for many' echo Isaiah's saying of the Servant who 'bore the sin of many'. (Mk. 10,45; Isa. 53,12)

Some writers in recent years have emphasized the importance of the Servant concept as an interpretation of the meaning of Christ for the early church, because it stressed his suffering and reconciling work. 'Early Christianity preserved the memory that Jesus himself was conscious of having to realize the work of the *'ebed Yahweh.* In the Gospel of John we find Jesus designated "Lamb of God", the Aramaic equivalent of which also means "Servant of God".'[1]

In the book of Acts we read that 'God has glorified his servant Jesus', and 'thy holy servant Jesus whom thou didst anoint'. (Acts 3,13; 3,26; 4,27; 4,30) This was translated by the Authorized Version as 'son', though when the same word was used of David it was rendered 'servant'. (Acts 4,25) But the Greek word used here (*pais*) was taken by the Greek translators of the Servant-poems in Isaiah to render *'ebed Yahweh.* There is another Greek word (*doulos*) which means 'slave', and this is never used directly of Jesus in the New Testament, though Paul once says that Jesus 'took the form of a slave'. (Phil. 2,7)

It seems that the Servant-concept was not uncommon in early Christianity, and it is found in prayers and exhortations outside the New Testament, such as the Didaché or Teaching of the Apostles, and the epistles of Clement. The Didaché (9 and 10)

[1] Cullmann, *Christology*, p. 79.

speaks both of 'thy servant David' and 'thy servant Jesus', and of knowledge, faith and immortality 'made known to us through thy servant Jesus'. Clement (16 and 59), says Jesus was 'as a servant, as a root in a thirsty ground' (quoting Isaiah 53) and 'thy beloved servant' or son.

The use of the title Servant in early Christianity would have helped to explain the sufferings of Christ by linking them directly to those of the Suffering Servant in Isaiah. Yet this title came to be neglected, perhaps because the theology of Gentile Christianity was determined more by faith in the resurrection than by the memory of the sufferings of the Cross. Still, as Cullman says, 'this Christological designation [of Servant] deserves more attention in contemporary theology than it usually receives, not only because it is one of the oldest answers to the question who Jesus is, but also because it goes back to Jesus himself and therefore opens to us most clearly the secret of his self-consciousness'.[1]

The teaching about Jesus as Servant of God is for a particular purpose, and his significance can best be understood in the light of his function. If the third Quranic reference, quoted above, links up with his baptism, the first two may be taken as indicating something of that absolute surrender to the will of God, that true worship, which is a principal thread in guiding towards an understanding of the mystery of the sufferings of Jesus.

(c) Prophet (*nabī*)

Jesus is once called Prophet alone in the Qur'ān (19,31/30), but he is often named in company with other prophets and figures of old, most of whom are mentioned in the Bible. The Arabic word for prophet (*nabī*) is the same as the Hebrew (*nābī*), and doubtless came through Syriac and Aramaic. It seems to have been known to the Arabs long before the time of Muḥammad.[2]

Whereas, it will be seen, each people had its messenger (*rasūl*), the Qur'ān speaks of the prophets as appearing only among the 'People of the Book' (*ahl al-kitāb*). Later theologians distinguished between the two classes of envoys and took *nabī*

[1] Cullmann, *Christology*, p. 81.

[2] *Foreign Vocabulary of the Qur'ān*, p. 276.

to be of wider significance, speaking of great numbers of prophets, some said up to 224,000. 'The Qur'ān itself does not support such a distinction. If anything the Quranic evidence would seem to point the other way and suggest that the *nabī* was the narrower term, the prophet being a special class among messengers.'[1]

As in the Bible the prophet in the Qur'ān appears as a messenger of a particular kind, chosen for a special purpose with a message from God. The prophets brought the books of divine revelation, Tawrāh, Zabūr and Injīl (Law, Psalter and Gospel). Similarly Muḥammad brought 'an Arabic Qur'ān' to make the Arabs also a People of the Book. He was the 'prophet of the community' (*al-nabī al-ummī*), as some interpret it, though most Muslim commentators prefer to take this phrase as meaning 'the illiterate prophet'. Bell says, '"belonging to the community", but also probably implying lack of Scripture'. Arberry renders it, 'the Prophet of the common folk', (see 7,156/157, and also 2,73/78 and 3,69/75)

It would be tedious and beyond our purpose to list all the prophets who are mentioned in the Qur'ān and attention is limited to those that are named along with Jesus.

2,130/136: 'What has been given to Moses and Jesus and what has been given to the prophets from their Lord.'

Practically the same words are in 3,78/84.

4,161/163: 'We made suggestions to Noah and the prophets after him . . . and the Patriarchs, and Jesus.'

5,48–50/44–46: 'We have sent down the Torah containing guidance and light; by it the prophets who surrendered themselves gave judgement . . . In their footsteps we caused Jesus, son of Mary, to follow, confirming the Torah which was before him, and we gave him the Gospel, containing guidance and light.'

6,84f. lists eighteen Hebrew prophets, including Jesus, and says, 'these are they upon whom we have bestowed the Book, and the jurisdiction and the prophetic office'.

19,31/30: 'He hath bestowed on me the Book, and hath made me a prophet.'

[1] A. Jeffery, 'The Qur'ān as Scripture', in *The Muslim World*, xl, p. 115f.

33,7: 'We took from the prophets their pledge – and from thee, and from . . . Jesus, son of Mary.'

57,26: 'We formerly sent Noah and Abraham, and appointed the prophetic office and the Book to be in their posterity . . . In their footsteps we caused Jesus, son of Mary, to follow, and we gave him the Gospel.'

These verses show Jesus in the succession of the great Hebrew prophets and patriarchs, but Jesus and Abraham alone appear in all the lists. Jesus followed the Torah (the Old Testament Law) that they had, but he receives a new and named book, the Gospel (*Injīl*, Evangel). At his birth it was said that God would teach Jesus the Book and the Wisdom and the Torah and the Gospel. (3,43/48) Moses had brought the Torah for the Jews, but Jesus brought the Gospel and the Evidences, his teaching and the miracles and grace of his life.

That the Jews disputed the title of Jesus to be a prophet was known to early Islam. Ibn Isḥāq, telling of Muḥammad's debate with certain Jews said that they 'asked him about the apostles he believed in . . . When he mentioned Jesus, son of Mary, they denied that he was a prophet saying, "We do not believe in Jesus, son of Mary, nor in anyone who believes in him". So God sent down concerning them: "O Scripture folk, do you blame us for anything but our belief in God and what he has sent down to us and what was sent down aforetime and because most of you are evil-doers?" '[1] Bukhārī, in his collection of the traditions, said that the Apostle of God said, 'I am nearest of men to the Son of Mary. Between Jesus and me there has been no prophet.'

A few modern Muslim writers have suggested that Jesus should be regarded as a prophet for the Jews only, and have bolstered up this suggestion by the sole Biblical verse, 'I was not sent but to the lost sheep of the house of Israel'. (Matt. 15,24) But this occurs in the particularly Jewish Gospel of Matthew, has no parallel in the other Gospels, and is opposed by the other instances in which Jesus ministered to Samaritans, Romans, Phoenicians and Greeks. The Qur'ān does not support

[1] A. Guillaume, *The Life of Muhammad*, a translation of Ibn Isḥāq's Sīrat Rasūl Allāh, 1955, p. 268.

a restriction of the teaching of Jesus, which it regards as divinely given like its own message (see 10,38/37; 10,94). Jesus is not only called Prophet, but also Messenger and Messiah, 'a sign to all beings'. (21,91) Professor Ḥusaini says that Jesus is a prophet of a unique type.

Twenty-eight prophets are named in the Qur'ān and later Islam believed that there were many more. However six were dignified with special titles: Adam the Chosen of God (Ṣafīy Allah); Noah the Prophet of God (Nabī Allah); Abraham the Friend of God (Khalīl Allah); Moses the Converser with God (Kalīm Allah); Jesus the Spirit of God (Rūḥ Allah); and Muḥammad the Apostle of God (Rasūl Allah). Muḥammad was called the last and Seal (Khātam), the end of prophecy. The mystic Ibn 'Arabī said, 'Muḥammad is the Seal of the Prophets and Jesus is the Seal of the Saints'. Jesus has been revered in the Islamic world as a model of sanctity and poverty, and a modern prayer says that 'wandering as a pilgrim belongs to the Prophet of God, 'Īsā'.[1]

The prophetic title is given to some whom the Bible regards rather as patriarchs, such as Adam and Noah, but these like all prophets have a 'covenant' with God (33,7). All the Quranic prophets seem to be Biblical characters, though not all can be easily identified; for example Idrīs (19,57/56) has been taken as either Esdras or Enoch. The prophets are human rather than angels, and as in the Bible they are 'sent', being servants of God. They have the word of God put in their mouth, to warn, to give good tidings, to use parables, and to reveal God's secret knowledge. The prophets are accredited by signs and there will be a reckoning with them at the last day, 'we shall assuredly question those to whom a messenger has been sent, and we shall question those who have been sent' (7,5/6). 'On the day of resurrection he [Jesus] will be regarding them a witness.' (4,157/159)[2]

In the Gospels Jesus was called a prophet by those who first heard his teaching: 'he is a prophet like one of the old prophets'. Some said that he was John the Baptist risen again, 'others

[1] C. Padwick, *Muslim Devotions*, 1961, pp. 168f.; M. Hayek, *Le Christ de l'Islam*, p.19.
[2] cp. Jeffery, 'The Qur'ān as Scripture'.

Elijah, others one of the prophets'. (Mark 6,15; 8,28) Jesus accepted this title when he said that a prophet is not without honour except in his own country, and that it could not be that a prophet should perish out of Jerusalem. (Mark 6,4; Luke 13,33) But he clearly did not think of himself as only a prophet, for his apparent self-designation as Son of Man suggests a more significant figure. But he did have some of the ecstasy or exultation of the prophet at times, and he believed himself to have been 'sent' by God, who had given him the Gospel. (Luke 10,21; 4,18) Like the prophets of old Jesus was filled with the Spirit of God and spoke his message.

In the Fourth Gospel there seems to be an attempt to show Jesus as *the* prophet, fulfilling the prediction of Moses that God would raise up a prophet like himself. John the Baptist denies that he is himself 'the prophet'. And at the feeding of the multitude the people say, 'surely this must be the prophet that was to come into the world'. (Deut. 18,15; John 1,21; 6,14)

Much commoner titles for Jesus in the Gospels are Rabbi, ('great one') a term of respect used for teachers of the Law, and especially Teacher (didaskalos), which occurs twenty-four times. Luke uses the term Master (epistatés) six times of Jesus, and this perhaps shows that the earlier titles were felt to be inadequate. 'A primitive title becomes subject to strain and disintegration as the significance of his person is more fully appraised . . . We have in the titles "Prophet" and "the Prophet" names which passed out of use because they were felt to be inadequate.'[1]

Cullmann has argued that if the title of Prophet for Jesus died out in early Christianity, yet Jewish Christianity had held to it, and the disappearance of the conception of Jesus as the True Prophet is connected with the disappearance of Jewish Christianity. He quotes a fragment from the *Gospel according to the Hebrews*, which was used by Jewish Christians, though his quotation is incomplete. At the baptism not only does the Spirit say, 'in all the prophets was I waiting for thee that thou shouldst come, and that I might rest in thee', but also 'thou art my first begotten son'. This latter phrase needs careful handling, as we shall see later, but no doubt it is Messianic and based on

[1] *The Names of Jesus*, pp. 14, 17.

Psalm 2. The only other evidence given by Cullmann is the apocryphal *Preaching of Peter*, given in a late Pseudo-Clementine novel, where Jesus is called the 'True Prophet'. But this is late and of little value for Jewish Christianity. The real Clement of Alexandria said much earlier that the Preaching of Peter called Jesus 'Law and Word', and spoke of his coming, his cross, resurrection and ascension.[1]

For an interpretation of the person of Jesus, as Cullmann says, the title Prophet has the advantage of showing the relationship of Jesus to the prophets of the Old Testament. It avoided also the political associations of the title Messiah. But the office of Prophet needs to be combined with that of Messiah or Christ, and also with the Logos or Word which joins the work of the prophet to his person.

The disadvantage of using the title Prophet only, which neither Qur'ān nor Bible do, would be that it tends to isolate the preaching mission of Jesus from the full significance of his life and work. This early Christology, however, may have lingered on in Syria and even in Arabia. In Islam, says Cullmann, 'the figure of the Prophet lives on in a new form'. But the view of prophecy in Islam is conditioned by Muḥammad's own vocation, and the concept of the continuity of the revelation of the Word of God, in Law, Gospel and Qur'ān.

(d) Messenger (*rasūl*)

The title Messenger or Apostle (*rasūl*) is used ten times of Jesus in the Qur'ān:

2,81/87: 'Messengers after him and we gave Jesus, son of Mary, the Evidences.'

2,254/253: 'To some of these messengers we gave pre-eminence [or 'we have preferred'] over others: among them are some to whom God spoke, and he raised some of them in rank; we gave Jesus, son of Mary, the Evidences.'

3,43/49: 'A messenger to the children of Israel.'

3,46/53: 'The disciples replied, "We have . . . followed the messenger".'

[1] *Christology of the New Testament*, pp. 38f.; *Apocryphal New Testament*, pp. 5 and 16f.

4,156/157: 'Their saying: "We killed the Messiah, Jesus, son of Mary, the messenger of God".'

4,169/171: 'The Messiah, Jesus, son of Mary, is nothing but a messenger [or 'was only the messenger'] of God.'

5,79/75: 'The Messiah, son of Mary, is nothing but a messenger before whose time the messengers have passed away.'

5,111: 'I suggested to [or 'inspired'] the disciples: "Believe in Me and my messenger".'

57,27: 'We caused our messengers to follow, and we caused Jesus, son of Mary, to follow.'

61,6: 'Jesus, son of Mary, said: "O Children of Israel, I am God's messenger to you".'

The distinction between a Messenger and a Prophet is not easy, but it is doubtful whether it can be maintained, with the Encyclopaedia of Islam, that 'the apostle is at the same time a prophet, but the prophet is not at the same time an apostle'.[1] In fact, it seems that whereas every people has its messenger, the prophets named in the Qur'ān are all in the succession of Abraham or Adam: the Hebrew, Christian and Muslim prophetic tradition. In modern studies of comparative religion these three are often called the Prophetic religions, with Indian and Far Eastern religions as Wisdom religions.

That every community has a messenger is stated a number of times in the Qur'ān, and this is a valuable idea in enabling recognition to be given to other religions, as part of the general revelation of God, distinct from the special or prophetic revelations:

10,48/47: 'Each community has a messenger, and when their messenger comes, judgement is given between them with justice.'

13,8/7: 'Thou art only a warner, and for every people there is a guide.'

22,35/34: 'For every community we have appointed a pious rite.'

23,46/44: 'We sent our messengers, one after the other.'

There are many such passages. Messengers have been sent with 'suggestions' from God: 'messengers bringing good tidings

[1] art. *Rasūl*. But see G. Widengren, *Muḥammad the Apostle of God*, 1955, p. 77.

and warnings, so that the people should have no argument against God after (the coming of) the messengers.' (4,163/165) So Muḥammad was sent as a messenger, a warner of the future judgement, and a reminder of past messengers. 'Our messenger has come to you to make things clear for you at an interval among the messengers [i.e. 'at a time when there are no others'], lest ye should say: "Neither bringer of good tidings nor warner has come to us".' (5,22/19)

Jesus was sent as a messenger, in succession to the earlier messengers. He ate food as they did, and died as they died (5,79/75; 19,34/33) Jesus is the messenger of God, commended to the disciples by God himself; and the disciples followed him, though some of the Jews rejected him and tried to kill him. Christian Apostles are called Disciples (see p. 93).

Jesus is called 'only' or 'nothing but' a messenger. This is not meant to depreciate his mission, but to place him in the context of other missions from God before and after. The Qur'ān also says that 'Muḥammad is only a messenger; before him the messengers have passed away'. Gabriel also is called rasūl.

Some messengers are exalted above others, because of a particular divine task and grace. This was already said of those prophets who had special books entrusted to them: 'we have given some of the prophets preference over others, and to David we gave Psalms.' (17,57/55) Jesus is both prophet and messenger to whom 'We gave pre-eminence over others'. (2,254/253) He had both Gospel and Evidences. The Evidences seem to mean the miracles of Jesus, which are mentioned several times in the Qur'ān, but also his teaching (see later p. 90). Furthermore, Jesus was supported or confirmed by the Holy Spirit.

Many times in the Bible the messengers of God are spoken of. God constantly sent his angelic and human envoys, 'rising up early and sending them'. There is the famous prophecy: 'behold I send my messenger (*malāk*), and he shall prepare the way before me: and the Lord, whom ye seek, shall suddenly come to his temple'. (Malachi 3,1) In the Gospel this messenger is identified with John the Baptist, who is said to have announced in his turn, 'after me comes one who is mightier than I'. (Mk. 1,7) Jesus is called Apostle in Hebrews 3,1.

A curious Biblical phrase used of Jesus is 'he that cometh'. This occurs twice in the question asked by John the Baptist himself: 'are you the one who is to come, or are we to expect some other?' Again it is used at the entry of Jesus to Jerusalem in the cry, 'Blessings on him who comes as king'. (Lk. 7,19; 19,38) In John's Gospel Jesus is spoken of as 'the prophet that was to come into the world', and 'the Messiah, the Son of God, who was to come into the world'. (Jn. 6,14; 11,27) But the title is rare. It 'had only a brief and restricted currency in certain circles. It has a marked eschatological tone.'[1]

A messenger (ἄγγελος) in general in the New Testament may be a human messenger, like John the Baptist. But much more often it is a heavenly messenger, an angel, a word which translates the same Greek original. An angel brings good tidings, and Jesus also brought Good Tidings, the Gospel.

In Islam the title Messenger (*rasūl*), has been applied above all to Muḥammad, and this is in the constant witness or confession (*shahāda*): 'Muḥammad is the apostle (*rasūl*) of God'. Jesus is pre-eminently, indeed uniquely, the Messiah.

The great importance of the message of Jesus, the Gospel, is recognized in the Qur'ān. Its validity is nowhere denied, but rather confirmed. Christians possess accurate copies of it, as we shall show against later critics, for it is said that the Gospel is 'in their possession', so 'let the people of the Gospel judge by what God hath sent down therein'. (5,51/47; 7,156/157)

(e) Word (*kalima*)

Jesus is spoken of as Word in certain passages which need considering with care. Already in 3,34/39 the birth of John the Baptist is announced: 'God giveth thee tidings of Yaḥyā, confirming a word from God.' This might seem to be a previous word or prophecy, though there is no mention of it earlier. Baiḍāwī commented on this: 'who shall confess to a word from God; i.e. Jesus, called "a word", because he came into existence by God's command without a father, so that he resembled the new creations, who are the world of command.' The Gospel, of course, does show John the Baptist confessing to Christ. (Jn.

[1] *The Names of Jesus*, p. 79.

1,29; 3,28f.) Rāzī said that Jesus 'was called a word' because he was the fulfilment of the word spoken to the prophets.

This Quranic passage then proceeds to announce the birth of Jesus: 'O Mary, God giveth thee tidings of a word from himself [Arberry, 'good tidings of a Word from Him'] whose name is the Messiah, Jesus.' (3,40/45) When Mary asks how this can be she is told that when God 'decideth upon a thing he simply saith "Be!" and it is'. At the end of this passage (3,52/59) Jesus is compared with Adam: 'Jesus in God's eyes is in the same position as Adam: He created him of dust, then said to him "Be!" and he is.'

That Jesus is a 'word from God' is affirmed again in 4,169/171: 'O People of the Book, do not go beyond bounds in your religion, and do not say about God anything but the truth. The Messiah, Jesus, son of Mary, is only the messenger of God, and his word which he cast upon Mary, and a spirit from him.' Arberry renders it, 'His Word which he committed to Mary, and a Spirit from Him'. This verse seems to be directed against certain Christian heresies, and particularly against the crude notion that God had carnally begotten Jesus upon Mary. In contrast to this it is declared that Jesus is born by the divine will and word.

Ibn Isḥāq, in his life of Muḥammad, said that the Muslim refugees in Abyssinia told the Christian emperor there that they believed that Jesus was the servant of God, 'and his apostle, and his spirit, and his word, which he cast into Mary the blessed virgin'. The Negus almost agreed with them.[1]

19,35/34 reads: 'That is Jesus, son of Mary – a statement of the truth concerning which they are in doubt.' It has often been remarked that with a slight change of vowel pointing this 'statement of truth' (*qawla'l-ḥaqqi*) could be read as 'word of truth' (*qawlu'l-ḥaqqi*), namely, that Jesus is the word of truth concerning which or whom men are in doubt. Since the original Qur'ān had no vowel points there is ambiguity in the reading; in addition there are numerous variants on this verse in old versions of the Qur'ān.[2]

[1] *The Life of Muhammad*, p. 152.

[2] See R. C. Zaehner, *At Sundry Times*, 1958, pp. 201ff.; A. Jeffery, *Materials for the History of the Text of the Qur'ān*, 1937.

It is significant that 19,36/35 goes on to say that God does not 'take to himself' offspring, 'he simply says "Be!" and it is'. Here again it is the creative word of God. We shall see the bearing of this later on the teaching of the virgin birth.

Some modern commentators have suggested that speaking of Jesus as 'word' means that he is a 'prophecy', or that he comes 'with a word'. But this appears to be inadequate. Jesus both comes as the effect of the word of God and is the word which God 'cast' (*alqā*) upon Mary. The older commentators saw this more clearly. Ṭabarī remarked, 'God calls this son which is in thy womb his word.' Rāghib said that Jesus is here called Word (*kalima*) in the sense in which the Prophet was later called Reminder (*dhikr*). However others said that 'the Word' was that which was cast into Mary, and Jesus was not himself that 'Be!'

Later Muslim writings sometimes referred to Jesus as he 'who was the Spirit and the Word, Jesus, son of Mary', and 'Jesus is God's Spirit and Word, his servant and his apostle'. So he was addressed in story as, 'O Spirit and Word of God.'[1]

It is well known that in the New Testament the Word (Logos) is one of the most significant titles applied to Christ. Yet it occurs only in the opening words of the Gospel and first epistle of John. Behind the word Logos of the Fourth Gospel there is no doubt the use made of it by the Jew Philo of Alexandria, just before the Christian writings. For Philo the Logos was the Divine Reason, intermediate between God and the world. This is a development of the concept of Wisdom in the Old Testament and apocrypha: wisdom was 'set up from everlasting', and was 'a breath of the power of God'. (Prov. 8, Wisdom 7) Proverbs shows Wisdom present in creation, 'I was by him as a master workman'.

It is significant that the Logos in John is linked with creation: 'in the beginning was the Word, the Word was with God, the Word was divine . . . all things were made through him.' This looks back to the first creation story in Genesis 1. There the universe and man were created not by crude fashioning with

[1] J. Robson, *Christ in Islam*, pp. 67, 123; M. Hayek, *Le Christ de l'Islam*. See also M. S. Seale, *Muslim Theology*, 1964, p. 110.

hands and dust, but by the sole creative word of God: 'God said', 'he spoke and it was done'. The Greek word Logos is one of the words used in the Septuagint Greek translation of the Old Testament to render the Hebrew *dābār*; for example, 'by the word [*dābār, logos*] of God the heavens were made'. (Ps. 33,6)

The word Logos is not used again of Christ in the New Testament, apart from 1 John 1 and Rev. 19,13, though similar ideas are found in Colossians 1 and Hebrews 1. In later development of the doctrine of Christ the Logos concept was found useful, up to the fourth century, but it declined after that and did not find its way into the major creeds or confessional documents. This may have been due to the use of Logos by various Gnostic sects. The apocryphal Acts of John, about the second century, contains a remarkable account of a dance in which the disciples 'going round in a ring', said to Jesus, 'Glory be to thee, Word: Glory be to thee, Grace: Glory be to thee, Spirit.'[1] This same Acts of John says that Jesus was only crucified in appearance, while he spoke in spirit to John (see later, p. 109f.).

A revival of the use of the Logos-doctrine has been suggested today, as a means of approach to people in other lands to whom a Word of God has clearly been spoken. 'If its inhabitants have enough serious purpose in them to want to talk to him about religion, or to listen to what he has to say about Christ, they have already within themselves encountered the Divine Logos.'[2]

(f) Spirit (*rūḥ*)

The use of the word Spirit in the Qur'ān is obscure, says the Encyclopaedia of Islam. But it occurs in connexion with Jesus seven times:

2,81/87: 'We gave Jesus, son of Mary, the Evidences, and aided him by the Spirit of Holiness' (or 'confirmed him with the Holy Spirit').

2,254/253 virtually the same: 'supported him by the Spirit of Holiness.'

[1] *The Apocryphal New Testament*, p. 253; B. Altaner, *Patrology*, p. 76.
[2] A. C. Bouquet, *The Christian Faith and Non-Christian Religions*, 1958, p. 160.

4,169/171: 'Jesus, son of Mary is . . . his word which he cast upon Mary, and a spirit from him.'

5,109/110: 'O Jesus, I supported thee by the Spirit of Holiness' (or 'I confirmed thee with the Holy Spirit').

19,17: 'Then we sent unto her [Mary] our spirit.'

21,91: 'So we breathed into her some of our spirit.'

66,12: 'We breathed into her some of our spirit.'

These verses show, first, that the Spirit was said to be active in the birth of Jesus, and this recalls Luke's Gospel: 'the Holy Spirit shall come upon thee', addressed to Mary. (Lk. 1,35)

Similar words are said about the creation of Adam: 'I have formed him, and breathed my spirit into him'. (15,29; 32,8/9; 38,72) This recalls Genesis 2,7: 'The Lord God . . . breathed into his nostrils the breath of life.'

Not only at his birth, according to the Qur'ān, but in the cradle, in youth, and as a grown man, the Holy Spirit supported Jesus. So the Gospel spoke of the descent of 'the Spirit like a dove' at the baptism, and of the beginning of his ministry 'armed with the power of the Spirit', whereby Jesus performed his mighty works. (Mk. 1,10; Lk. 4,14)

While the support of the Spirit is said, in those words, to be given to Jesus, and this is repeated three times in the Qur'ān, yet there are others who are aided by the Spirit. Of all believers it is said that, 'He hath inscribed faith on their hearts, and hath supported them with a Spirit from himself'. (58,22) Like the Evidences and the Gospel, the Qur'ān comes down through the Spirit, 'the Spirit of Holiness has sent it down from the Lord'. (16,104/102) The mediator of the word may be 'Gabriel – verily he hath brought it down' (2,91/97), but the Spirit comes with it, 'verily it is a revelation of the Lord of the worlds, with which hath come down the faithful Spirit'. (26,192)

Most intriguing is sūra 4,169/171, quoted above, in which Jesus is spoken of as 'a spirit from' God. Some commentators have suggested that spirit (*rūḥ*) could also mean 'mercy' and so Jesus would be a 'mercy from God'; but mercy is normally *raḥma*. Then if *rūḥ* were taken as 'inspiration' or 'divine revelation', this could give the rendering of Jesus as 'a prophecy which God communicated to Mary'. Finally it is said that

Jesus is called 'a spirit' and not 'the spirit', and the word is not used exclusively of him.[1] But another modern commentator says bluntly that 'Christ was a spirit proceeding from God'.[2]

The fact is that Muslim writers have spoken of Jesus as 'the Spirit' and 'Spirit of God'. Ibn Isḥāq quoted a letter sent from Muḥammad to the Negus of Abyssinia in which the Prophet said, 'I bear witness that Jesus son of Mary is the spirit of God and his word which he cast to Mary the virgin.' Ibn 'Arabī said that God had reserved to Jesus being Spirit, and gave him this extra gift of life-giving breath.[3]

In later Muslim story the disciples asked Jesus, 'Explain to us, O Spirit of God, the difference between love for your friend and love for your Lord'; and again, 'O Spirit of God, describe to us the friends of God'. The title occurs in various narratives, of which a well-known one tells of Jesus speaking to a skull, which in return talks to him: 'O Spirit of God I was a king . . . O Spirit of God, I belonged to a people with whom God was angry . . . O Spirit of God, you have named the best of names'. From another Muslim source came a story of Jesus sending James, Thomas and Peter to announce his coming to the king of Nasibin. They entered the city and cried out, 'Jesus the Prophet of God and the Spirit of God has come to the city'.[4]

It was said earlier that in lists of prophets who had brought new dispensations Jesus had the special title of Spirit of God. This is not just past custom but it is present practice also. Miss Padwick has collected samples of the popular list-prayers which praise the prophets in turn, and in a 'favourite and endlessly reprinted devotion of Indian Muslims' comes the regular mention of 'Īsā the Spirit of God. Many other list-prayers call down blessing on the prophets 'and on the Spirit of God 'Īsā the Faithful'.[5]

It is remarkable, then, that the title Spirit was not applied to Jesus in the Bible. The Arabic *rūḥ* is related of course to the Hebrew *ruach*, which is rendered in the New Testament by

[1] M. 'Alī, *Holy Qur'ān*, p. 234.
[2] Yusuf 'Alī, commentary on the Qur'ān, Lahore, 1934, p. 234. But others say that 'the Spirit was sent on him by divine command'. See M. S. Seale, *Muslim Theology*, p. 111.
[3] *Life of Muhammad*, p. 657; *Le Christ de l'Islam*, p. 89.
[4] *Christ in Islam*, pp. 54, 86, 102.
[5] *Muslim Devotions*, pp. 168f.

pneuma and used of wind, breath, a spirit, and the Holy Spirit. The Holy Spirit is the divine presence and power, which descended upon Jesus in his humanity. Occasionally mystical language brought the Spirit of God and the Spirit of Christ close together. (Romans 8,9) And in the first chapter of John the idea of the Word is not unlike that of the divine Spirit working in the world. But of course the closest verse to sura 4,169/171 ('a spirit from him') is in the annunciation story, 'the Holy Spirit shall come upon thee'. (Lk. 1,35) It is not necessary to go any further than this in speculation.

Some modern writers have pointed out the close connexion between the Spirit and the Command or Affair (*amr*) of God:

17,87/85: 'They ask thee about the Spirit; say: "The Spirit belongs to my Lord's affair" ' (or 'the Spirit is of the bidding of my Lord').

16,2: 'He sendeth down the angels with the spirit (which is) part of his affair upon whomsoever he willeth of his servants' (or 'he sends down the angels with the Spirit of his command').

Amr is from the same root as the Hebrew *memrā*, which corresponds to the Greek Logos or Word. It is used in two senses, of a command or decree, and of a matter or affair. Though a genuinely Arabic word, when used in connexion with the doctrine of revelation in the Qur'ān 'the whole conception seems to have been strongly influenced by the Christian Logos doctrine, though the word would seem to have arisen from the Targumic use of *memrā*.[1] The later complexity of the use of the word Spirit shows the difficulty of expressing the mystery of God and his revelation and action through his Word and through his Spirit.

(g) Other titles of Jesus

A Sign (*āya*)

This word was probably borrowed from Syriac or Aramaic, and although used frequently in the Qur'ān it only comes occasionally in the early Meccan passages. Later it was used to indicate verses of the Qur'ān, but in the scripture itself it seems to mean

[1] *Foreign Vocabulary of the Qur'ān*, p. 69; R. C. Zaehner, *At Sundry Times*, pp. 214f.; J. W. Sweetman, *Islam and Christian Theology*, 1945, i, p. 29; J. M. S. Baljon, 'The *amr* of God in the Koran', *Acta Orientalia*, 1958.

simply a sign. Jesus was such a sign not only to the Israelites but to the world.

19,21: 'We may make him a sign to the people' (or 'a sign unto men').

21,91: 'Made her and her son a sign to the worlds' (or 'to all beings', Arberry).

23,52/50: 'We appointed the Son of Mary and his mother to be a sign.'

And in 3,44/50 Jesus comes to the children of Israel with 'a sign from your Lord'.

A Parable or Example (*mathal*)

This is like the Hebrew *māshāl* which is rendered parable (*parabolē*) in the New Testament and means an analogy, figure or example.

43,57: 'The Son of Mary is used as a parable' or 'cited as an example'.

43,59: 'We ... have appointed him to be a parable for the Children of Israel' (or 'an example to the Children of Israel').

See 3,52/59: 'The likeness (*mathal*) of Jesus ... is as Adam's likeness' (or 'in the same position as Adam').

A Witness (*shahīd*)

4,157/159: 'On the day of resurrection he will be regarding them a witness.'

5,117: 'I was a witness over them as long as I remained amongst them.'

The Qur'ān teaches that at the judgement each community will have a witness, and 'woe to those who have disbelieved because of the witnessing of a mighty day' (see 4,45/41; 19,38; 28,75). 'The Witness' is one of the Beautiful Names of God and occurs frequently in the Qur'ān (e.g. 4,37/33).

A Mercy (*raḥma*)

19,21: 'A mercy from us.'

Eminent (*wajīh*)

3,40/45: 'An eminent one in this world and the hereafter' or 'high honoured in this world and the next'.

Baiḍāwī said that the eminence in this world was in the prophetic office of Jesus and in the next the right of intercession. But this comes in the Annunciation story, and parallels Luke 1,32, 'He shall be great . . . and of his Kingdom there shall be no end.'

One brought near (*min al-muqarrabīn*)

3,40/45: 'One of those brought near' or 'near stationed to God'. (Arberry).

Baiḍāwī said that according to some what was intended here was the high place that Jesus was to have in paradise, or his being raised to heaven into the society of angels. Later Islam sometimes explained this of the state of Jesus after his ascension, in one of the heavens. Ibn Isḥāq says in the story of Muḥammad's vision of heaven that he saw Jesus, son of Mary, in the second heaven, perhaps awaiting his return. Sura 56,11 speaks of those who go before, in gardens of delight, 'they are those brought near', and see 7,111/114.

One of the upright (*min al-ṣāliḥīn*)

3,40/46: 'One of the upright' or 'righteous shall he be'.

The same is said of John the Baptist in 3,34/39.

Blessed (*mubarak*)

19,32/31: 'Blessed wherever I am.'

Baiḍāwī explained this as 'possessing much profit for others', apparently as possessing a *baraka*, a blessed power. See also 19,34/33: 'Peace is upon me the day of my birth', and in 43,59 Jesus is one 'on whom we have bestowed favour'.

It has been remarked (p. 46) that 19.35 says, 'that is Jesus, Son of Mary – a statement of the truth'. In his note Bell points out that the slight change of pointing could give 'the Word of Truth', referring to Jesus. Some translators have accepted this (Sale, Zaehner, etc.). But Muslim commentators have taken the words to mean 'a statement of truth, closing the account of the annunciation against Jewish slanders'. Bell accepts this in his text. A similar phrase is found after the first account of the annunciation in 3,53/60: 'the truth from thy Lord, so be not of those who doubt.'

5

Zachariah and John

ZACHARIAH and his son John the Baptist are both mentioned several times in the Qur'ān, and always in connexion with Jesus, so that to make this account complete the Quranic references to them will be given.

Zachariah (Zakarīyā') appears four times as the father of John, though in 3,32/37 he is the elder who took charge of Mary from childhood. The name probably came from Syria, and a like form is used by the Mandaeans. Muslim legend identified Zachariah with the martyr priest of 2 Chronicles 24,21, but this identification appeared already in the second century apocryphal Book of James. Ṭabarī said that Zachariah hid in a tree and was killed by being sawn in two.[1]

John the Baptist is called Yaḥyā, which some commentators said came from an Arabic word meaning 'to quicken', as John quickened his mother's barrenness and his people's faith. But Baiḍāwī admitted that it was a foreign form, and it may have come from a Christian or Christianized source, perhaps the Syriac Yoḥannan, and was naturalized among the early Arabs. It has been suggested that in early undotted Qur'āns the word could be read as either Yoḥanna or Yaḥyā.[2] The Mandaeans of Iraq and Iran still call John Yuhanā or Yaḥyā Yuhanā, but it seems likely that the Yaḥyā, like their form of Zākaria, has been influenced by Arabic. The Mandaeans regard John as a great

[1] *Apocryphal New Testament*, p. 48.

[2] *The Foreign Vocabulary of the Qur'ān*, pp. 290, 151; A. Mingana, *Syriac Influence on the Style of the Kur'ān*, p. 10.

teacher, a Naṣurai, that is, an adept in the faith; but they look on Jesus as a rebel or heretic, no doubt in reaction against Christians. They do not claim that their religion originated with John, as is sometimes said of them, but his use of river water in baptism would recommend him to them because of the Mandaean regard for 'living' or flowing water.[1]

In 6,85, a Meccan sūra, we read of 'Zachariah and Yaḥyā and Jesus and Elias – each one of the righteous'.

In 21,89–90, late Meccan, before a reference to Mary and her son, we read: 'And Zachariah – when he called to his Lord: "O my Lord, leave me not solitary, though thou art the best of heirs". So we answered him, and gave him Yaḥyā, and made his spouse right for him.' This is the sūra of the Prophets, enumerating many of them, and ending with Mary and Jesus.

In sūra 3,32f./37f. Zachariah has charge of Mary in the temple (see next chapter) and then is promised John: 'There Zachariah called upon his Lord, and said: "O my Lord, give me from thyself a good offspring; verily thou art the hearer of prayer". So the angels called to him while he was yet standing praying in the sanctuary: "Verily God giveth thee tidings of Yaḥyā, confirming a word from God, a leader, abstinent, a prophet, one of the upright". Said he: "My Lord, how shall I have a youth, seeing that old age has come upon me and my wife is barren?" He replied: "So (shall it be), God doeth as he willeth". He said: "My Lord, appoint for me a sign". He replied: "Thy sign is that thou shalt not speak to the people for three days except by gesture; but remember thy Lord often and give glory in the evening and the morning".'

This is from the long Medinan sūra 3, which then continues with the annunciation to Mary and some teaching of Jesus. But the fullest account of the promise of John to Zachariah is in the Meccan (or Meccan based) sūra 19. This is the sūra of Mary, and the story of the annunciation to Mary and the nativity of Jesus is prefaced by fifteen verses on Zachariah and John. So sūra 19 reads:

1: 'Mention of the mercy of thy Lord to his servant Zachariah.
2/3: '(Recall) When he called upon his Lord secretly.

[1] E. S. Drower, *The Mandaeans of Iraq and Iran*, 1937, p. 3.

3/4: 'He said: "O my Lord, the strength has gone from my bone, and my head is lit up with white.

4: '"But I have not (hitherto) been in my prayer to thee, O my Lord, unfortunate.

5: '"Verily I have become afraid of the next-of-kin to come after me and my wife is barren; so give me from thyself a next-of-kin,

6: ' "To inherit me, and to inherit from the family of Jacob, and make him, O my Lord, well-pleasing".

7: ' "O Zachariah, We give thee good tidings of a boy whose name is Yaḥyā.

8/7: ' "To whom we have never before appointed a namesake."

9/8: 'Said he: "O my Lord, how shall I have a boy, seeing that my wife has become barren, and I have reached of age an advanced (degree)?"

10/9: 'Said he: "So shall it be! Thy Lord hath said: 'It is easy for me, seeing I have created thee formerly when thou wert nothing' ".

11/10: 'Said he: "O my Lord, appoint for me a sign".
Said he: "Thy sign is that thou shalt not speak to the people for three days [lit. 'nights'] exactly".

12/11: 'So he came forth to his people from the sanctuary [*miḥrāb*], and signed [or 'suggested'] to them "Give glory morning and evening".

13/12: ' "O Yaḥyā, take the Book with power"; and We gave him the jurisdiction as a child.

14/13: 'And grace from our side and purity [*zakāt*, alms, or purity and virtue], and he was pious, and dutiful towards his parents, and was not a tyrant, rebellious.

15: 'Peace is upon him the day of his birth, and the day of his death, and the day of his being raised up alive.'

This passage is close to the Gospel (Luke 1,5–25), but it should be noted that here, and in the story of Mary and the nativity, it is Luke rather than Matthew that provides the parallel. There is no need to relate the Gospel story at length: Zachariah was a priest, his wife was barren, the angel Gabriel promised him a son while he was praying in the temple, and because of Zachariah's doubts he became dumb for nine months till the child was born and named John by his father.

Nothing more need be said of Zachariah for the moment, he has his part to play as father of John and patron of Mary, in the Qur'ān. In later Muslim legend he died as a martyr, and it is said that his tomb is in Damascus.

Some interesting things are said of John. His name was regarded as new (19,8/7), perhaps meaning that none of his relatives had borne this name (as in Lk. 1,61). His birth came 'confirming a word from God', and by the power of the divine word, 'So shall it be'; for creation is easy to God who made man out of nothing. John is called a leader (*sayyid*) which commentators take to mean merciful, for 19,14/13 says that John was pious and dutiful towards his parents, and not a tyrant or rebellious. John is called a prophet and 'one of the upright', like Jesus (3,34–41/39–46). His 'abstinence' recalls the Gospel saying that he should 'drink no wine nor strong drink'. (Lk. 1,15)

Of interest is the command addressed to John: 'O Yaḥyā, take the Book with power.' (19,13/12) This might seem to suggest that John had a special revealed book, but there is no other reference to this and the commentators consider that the book here mentioned is the Torah, for John's mission was to confirm the word of God. (3,34/39) Zamakhsharī said that God gave John understanding of the Torah, and this was the wisdom or jurisdiction granted to him as a child.

The Qur'ān says no more of the mission and life of John the Baptist, though it invokes peace upon his birth, death and resurrection in terms closely similar to those used about Jesus (19,15 and 19,34/33). There is no need to speak of his birth as 'miraculous' or of him speaking 'in his cradle', as the Encyclopaedia of Islam asserts. Like other prophets John was upright and pious, his birth came after a divine promise, like those of Isaac and Samuel, but in the normal processes of human generation.

Later Islam had various stories and legends of John. Ṭabarī said that John was the first to believe in Jesus; and while the Gospel had shown him believing yet elsewhere he seemed to express doubts. (John 1,29: Lk. 7,19) The story of his death at the request of Herodias is variously given. His reputed tomb is still shown in the great mosque of Damascus. The Mandaeans, sometimes called 'Christians of St John', have occasionally been identified with the Sabaeans who are three times mentioned in the Qur'ān (2,59/62; 5,73/69; 22,17) along with Jews and Christians as 'people of the book'. But it seems more likely that the Sabaeans were pagan monotheists of Mesopotamia who were mentioned with interest by Arabic writers from the fourth Islamic century onwards. They may well have had points of common belief with the orthodox Mandaeans whose rituals are close to ancient Zoroastrian practices (see p. 153).

6

Mary (Maryam)

Mary, the mother of Jesus, is the only woman who is called by her proper name in the Qur'ān. Other women are mentioned but not named: the wives of Noah, Lot, Pharaoh (66,10–12), 'Imrān, Zachariah (3,30–35/33–40), and the Queen of Sheba (27,22ff.). Most of these are unnamed in the Bible also. Mary's mother is not named in either Bible or Qur'ān, though apocryphal writings soon found a name for her.

The name Maryam comes from Hebrew and Aramaic as Baiḍāwī admitted, though the vowelling of the Arabic points to a Christian source, probably Syriac. There seems no evidence that it was used in Arabia in pre-Islamic times. Muḥammad at Medina was sent a Coptic Christian concubine with the notably different name form of Māriyah; in Ethiopic both syllables are long – Māryām.

The Qur'ān uses the name Mary more times than does the New Testament; thirty-four times in the former, nineteen times in the latter. However twenty-three of these Quranic instances occur in the title Son of Mary, and there are more stories about Mary in the Bible, since she is sometimes called 'mother of Jesus' there without using her proper name. Neither in the Bible nor the Qur'ān is she called the Virgin Mary, the title of later Christian reverence, though these scriptures may well assume her virginity.

Mary and Jesus are 'a sign to the worlds'. (21,91) But, as in the Gospel, the importance of Mary for the Qur'ān is in being mother to Jesus. She has no role to play apart from that, and in both scriptures the attitude of Mary is one of humble acceptance of the part God assigned to her: 'prostrate thyself' (3,38/43), and 'Behold the servant of the Lord'. (Lk. 1,38) This submission, surrender to the will of God, is fundamental to both Quranic and Biblical religion and the key to understanding some of its deepest mysteries.

Since the Quranic stories are long, it is convenient to deal here separately with the preliminary accounts of Mary, and to consider the annunciation and birth of Jesus later though, of course, these form an integral part of the story of Mary. That story is one in which Mary is consistently honoured.

66,10–12 gives examples of unbelievers and believers, the wives of Noah and Lot who disbelieved, and Pharaoh's wife and Mary who believed: 'Mary, the daughter of 'Imrān, who guarded her chastity [lit. 'private parts'], so We breathed into them ['her'] some of our Spirit, and she counted true the words of her Lord and his Books, and became one of the devout'. The variant reading 'into her' or 'into him' (*fīhi*) has been taken by some (e.g. Rāzī) to refer to Jesus receiving the spirit; but sura 19,17 says also 'we sent to her our spirit' (and see 21,91).

From the first Meccan period comes 23,52/50: 'We appointed the Son of Mary and his mother to be a sign, and we made them repair to a height with a secure abode [or 'a hollow'] and a spring.' 21,91, also Meccan, says: 'She who guarded her chastity – so we breathed into her some of our spirit and made her and her son a sign to the worlds' (or 'all beings').

Various points to be noted here will be considered below. But Mary is defended against attacks. Jewish speaking against her was 'a mighty slander'. (4,155/156) She was 'a faithful woman'. (5,79/75) When she carried her baby home and was suspected of improper behaviour, the child himself justified her and said, 'I am the servant of God'. (19,28f.) Twice she is said to have kept her purity, and twice more she protests her virginity when the birth is foretold.

Down the ages the purity of Mary has been cherished. Already Ibn Isḥāq spoke of 'Mary the virgin, the good, the pure'.[1] The female Ṣūfī mystic Rābi'a was called 'a second

[1] *Life of Muhammad*, p. 657.

spotless Mary'. Later Islam regarded Mary as sinless, in company with all the prophets, and a basis for belief in Mary's sinlessness was found in sūra 3,31/35 where Mary's mother said: 'I seek refuge with thee for her and her progeny from Satan the stoned.' On this Bukhārī gave a tradition of Muḥammad saying that no child of Adam is born without a demon touching him at the moment of birth. The one whom the demon touches gives out a cry, which is why all children cry. There have been no exceptions but Mary and her son. Later legend added that Gabriel touched Jesus with his wing at birth to save him from contact with Satan. But these stories are too unnatural or superhuman, like the hymn which says that 'little Lord Jesus no crying he makes'. Commentators may have felt that objection when they interpreted this verse to mean that Satan desires to mislead all children, except Mary and her son who were protected by this invocation. But even this does not get to the root of the verse which is the religious action of going to God for refuge against all evil. And there may be a further link with the Gospel story of the temptation of Jesus by Satan, which he overcame; Matt. 4,10. See also Sura 22,51/52, 'We sent not ever any Messenger or Prophet before thee, but that Satan cast into his fancy'.

The human needs of Mary are affirmed in the Qur'ān along with those of Jesus: 'both of them ate food'. (5,79/75) This may have been said partly in defence of Muḥammad, who was criticized for 'eating food and going about the market-places'. (25,8/7, etc.) To vulgar legend true prophets seemed too sublime to need food, and so the Qur'ān asserted that 'we have not sent before thee any of the envoys but they ate food'. (25,22/20) Some early Christians also had accepted Docetic views, thinking that Jesus was simply an 'appearance' (from *dokein*, to seem) who had no mortal needs. This heresy needed contradiction.

There is a difficult Quranic verse (5,116) which will be considered further when discussing the doctrine of the Trinity: 'God said: "O Jesus, son of Mary, was it thou who didst say to the people: 'Take me and my mother as two gods apart from God?'"' Jesus is said to have denied this indignantly, and it must be simply stated here that such a statement would be a Christian as well as an Islamic heresy.

Yet there was undoubtedly a tendency in this direction in the Christianity of that time. In the fifth century Nestorius, patriarch of Constantinople, had protested against the growing use of the title 'Mother of God' (*theotokos*, god-bearer) applied to Mary. He said that it should be 'mother of the man' Jesus (*anthropo-tokos*), or 'mother of Christ' (*christo-tokos*). Nestorius also refused to admit the use of such phrases as that 'God was born' and 'God suffered', which were in current use. He taught that the man Jesus was the organ, vessel or temple of the Son of God. The Nestorian churches eventually separated on this issue; they were found in Antioch and the east, became great missionaries over a large part of Asia, and seem to have been preferred by Muslims to the rival Monophysite school of Alexandria.

The Meccan sūra 19 tells the story of the annunciation to Mary and the nativity. But the later Medinan sūra 3 has some preliminary matter, which can be given here.

3,30/33: 'Verily God hath chosen Adam and Noah, the family of Abraham and the family of 'Imrān above the worlds ['above all beings']; descendants one of the other, God is one who hears and knows.

3,31/35: '(Recall) when the wife of 'Imrān said: "O my Lord, I vow to thee what is in my belly, dedicated (to thy service); accept (it) from me, verily thou art one who hears and knows". Then when she was delivered of it, she said: "O my Lord, what I have been delivered of is a female"; – God knew quite well what she had been delivered of; the male is not like the female – "I have named her Mary, and I seek refuge with thee for her and her progeny from Satan the stoned" (or "to protect them from the accursed Satan").

3,32/37: 'So her Lord vouchsafed her a good acceptance, and caused her to shoot up a goodly growth (or 'by his goodness she grew up comely'). Zachariah took charge of her. Whenever Zachariah entered the sanctuary to see her, he found beside her provisions. Said he: "O Mary, how hast thou this?" She replied: "It is from God; God provides for whom he willeth without reckoning".'

The sūra then continues with the announcement of Yaḥyā to Zachariah, already quoted in the last chapter, and then the annunciation of Jesus which will be treated in the next chapter.

The title of sūra 3 is 'Imrān, or the House or Family of 'Imrān. Here, and in 66,12, Mary is called the daughter of 'Imrān. According to the Bible 'Amrām was the father of Moses, Aaron and Miriam. (Num. 26,59) The ultimate source of the name 'Imrān would seem to be Hebrew, through Syriac, though there may have been an early Arabic form taken from Jewish or Christian sources. There may appear to be a blending of Mary, mother of Jesus (called Maryam in Qur'ān and Greek Gospel) with Miriam, daughter of 'Amrām. And sura 19,29/28, addressing Mary, reads: 'O sister [or 'daughter'] of Aaron' (but see later, p. 78).

Sūra 3,30/33 however speaks of descent from the four patriarchs Adam, Noah, Abraham and 'Imrān, and Muslim commentators generally take this passage to mean that Mary was of Levitical race, descended from 'Amrām, or that there was another 'Imrān later. So Baiḍāwī said that between the two 'Imrāns there were 1800 years, while Ṭabarī said that Zachariah had a cousin called 'Imrān.

Christian apocrypha called Mary's father Joachim and her mother Anna. Baiḍāwī accepted this name of Anna for Mary's mother and he recounted a story, found in the early apocryphal Book of James, that when Anna was sitting under a tree watching a bird feed its young she lamented her barrenness, and promised that if God would give her a child she would devote it to the service of God in the temple. He explained 3,31/35 (above) by saying that Anna perhaps made the vow on the assumption that it would be a male child, hence her exclamation: 'O my Lord, what I have been delivered of is a female.' But 'God knew best', for he knew the worth of the child Mary, and 'he vouchsafed to her a good acceptance', meaning that he was satisfied with her in place of a male for the fulfilment of the vow. The child Samuel, son of Hannah in the Old Testament, had been promised to the service of God before his birth. Mary could not be a priest because of her sex, but it was just that which fitted her for the appointed task of giving birth to Jesus

There is no Biblical parallel for the child Mary being cared for in the temple (*miḥrāb*, sanctuary, niche or cell; see 19,11) or by Zachariah, though in her pregnancy Mary did go to stay for three months in Zachariah's house. (Lk. 1,40–56) According to the Book of James Mary was taken to the temple at three years old, where Zachariah was priest, and 'she received food from the hand of an angel'.[1] Baiḍāwī commented on 3,32/37, where Zachariah found provisions beside Mary, that Mary never sucked the breast, for her nourishment was sent down from heaven. He even added that Zachariah used to lock seven doors upon Mary, and yet would find the fruits of summer by her in winter. But some modern Muslim writers object to finding miraculous food here. Food 'from God', they say, need not mean that Mary's food came direct from God without human intermediary, for ordinary believers may speak of their food in this way. It is considered that Mary was fed by gifts left by worshippers in the temple.[2]

It is convenient here to anticipate sura 3,39/44, since it continues the same narrative:

> 'That is one of the stories of the unseen, which we give thee by inspiration; thou wast not with them when they cast their pens (to decide) which of them should take charge of Mary, nor wast thou with them when they were contending.'

This seems to continue the story of Mary in the temple and Baiḍāwī interpreted it of priests casting lots with the pens with which they wrote the Law, to decide who should be Mary's guardian. The Book of James makes Zachariah call the widowers of Israel each to bring a rod, to decide whose wife Mary should be. Joseph was chosen and took Mary home, though he was old, but later she returned to the temple for the annunciation.

The Book of James is one of the oldest Christian apocrypha, upon which many others depend, adding to its stories. Most of this must be regarded as legend, and there is little evidence of any historical fact apart from that which is derived from the Gospel. The Gospel is very reserved in its stories of Mary, and

[1] *Apocryphal New Testament*, pp. 40ff.
[2] J. M. S. Baljon, *Modern Muslim Koran Interpretation*, 1961, p. 22.

it has not that riot of hagiography which grew up with the glorification of Mary for her own sake, rather than as the mother of Jesus and servant of the Lord.

The Prophet Muḥammad had a deep veneration for Mary as mother of Jesus. The oldest historian of Mecca, Azraqī, who died in A.D. 858, said that in the Ka'ba of Mecca, on the column nearest the door, was a picture of Mary with Jesus on her knee. When Muḥammad entered Mecca in triumph he gave orders to destroy the idols of the Ka'ba and its paintings of prophets and angels. But it is said that when his followers began to wash away the paintings with water from the Zamzam well, Muḥammad put his hands on the picture of Jesus and Mary and said, 'Wash out all except what is below my hands'.[1] Whether this story is true or not, there is no doubt that the Prophet showed the utmost respect for Jesus and his mother.

[1] *Encyclopaedia of Islam*, art. Ka'ba; K. A. C. Creswell, *A Short Account of Early Muslim Architecture*, 1958, p. 2.

7

The Annunciation

SŪRA 19 gives the longest version of the annunciation and birth of Jesus, though there are shorter references elsewhere.

19,16: 'Make mention in the book of Mary; when she withdrew from her people to a place, eastward.

19,17: 'And took between herself and them a curtain [or 'veil']. Then we sent to her our spirit, who took for her the form of a human being, shapely [or 'a man without fault'].

19,18: 'She said: "Lo, I take refuge with the Merciful from thee, if thou art pious [or 'if thou fearest God']".

19,19: 'He said: "I am the messenger of thy Lord, that I may give thee a boy, pure".

19,20: 'She said: "How shall I have a boy, seeing that man hath not touched me, nor have I been a harlot?"

19,21: 'He said: "So shall it be! Thy Lord hath said: 'It is easy for me', and (it is) in order that we may make him a sign for the people [or 'a sign unto men'], and a mercy from us; it has become a thing decided [or 'decreed']".'

Sura 3 says very much the same:

3,37/42: '(Recall) when the angels said: "O Mary, verily God hath chosen thee and purified thee, and chosen thee above the women of the worlds [or 'above all women'].

3,38/43: ' "O Mary, be obedient to thy Lord, prostrate thyself and bow with those who bow".'

Sura 3,39/44 has been given in the last chapter.

3,40/45: '(Recall) when the angels said: "O Mary, God giveth thee tidings of a word from himself whose name is the

Messiah, Jesus, son of Mary, an eminent one in this world and the hereafter, one of those brought near [or 'near stationed to God'].

3,41/46: ' "And he will speak to the people in the cradle and as grown man, one of the upright [or 'righteous shall he be']".

3,42/47: 'She said: "My Lord, how shall I have a child, seeing no man hath touched me?" He said: "So (shall it be), God createth what he willeth, when he decideth upon a thing, he simply saith 'Be!' and it is".'

Reference may be also made again to 21,91 and 66,12 which both speak of Mary, 'who guarded her chastity, so we breathed into her some of our spirit'.

Mary's withdrawing 'to a place eastward', and 'with a curtain' or veil, has found various explanations. The Book of James says that Mary was weaving a veil for the temple in her house when the angel came. Neither the Qur'ān nor the Bible situate the annunciation in the temple, and a modern interpreter, Maulana Āzād, said that the 'eastern place' is Nazareth which is 'corroborated by the New Testament'.[1]

The rest of the Quranic narratives quoted above agree closely with the Gospel according to Luke (except perhaps 3,41/46, speaking 'in the cradle', which will be considered in the next chapter on the nativity). The angel is not named in this connexion in the Qur'ān as Gabriel (Jibrīl), though he appears elsewhere in the Qur'ān as the angel of revelation, and commentators have assumed that it was he who appeared to Mary. In Luke the angel Gabriel comes to Mary at Nazareth and salutes her as 'highly favoured, the Lord is with thee' ('blessed art thou among women' was added by some ancient authorities, and no doubt would become widely known). Mary was troubled at the salutation and was told not to be afraid for she would bear a son and call his name Jesus. She asked how this could be, 'seeing I know not a man?' The angel replied that 'the Holy Spirit shall come upon thee, and the power of the Most High shall overshadow thee'. The example of Elizabeth conceiving a child in her old age was quoted as confirmation that 'no word

[1] *Modern Muslim Koran Interpretation*, p. 86.

of God shall be void of power'. Mary then submitted: 'Behold the handmaid of the Lord; be it unto me according to thy word' (Lk. 1,26ff.)

The Qur'ān firmly refutes any suggestion of unchastity by Mary, or any divine coupling with a woman such as might suggest ancient classical or Arabian myths of the ways of the gods. But the commentators have not been free from speculation that is more legendary than scriptural. Ṭabarī in his chronicle said that Gabriel was sent to Mary that he might blow into her sleeve and that she might conceive, apparently thus receiving the spirit. Baiḍāwī repeated this idea of Gabriel breathing into Mary's chemise. Ṭabarī said that Gabriel showed himself to Mary in the form of Joseph the carpenter, for Mary had never seen any man except Zachariah and Joseph. When Gabriel said that he would give her a son, she was afraid that Joseph had come to have intercourse with her. But Gabriel said that God wished to create the child without a father and make him a prophet. This is vulgar legend which has no scriptural warrant.

According to the Qur'ān the birth of Jesus would be brought about by the plain but all-powerful word of God. 'He simply saith, "Be [*kun*]!" and it is.' The might of the divine speech and decree is a principal theme of the Qur'ān. It is in accord with the Biblical view of the creation, where 'God spoke, and it was done'. For this reason no doubt the birth of Jesus is compared with that of Adam, both were by divine decree and power (see 2, 110).

In the past it was usually assumed that the Qur'ān taught the virgin birth of Jesus. Some Christian apologists suggested that the immaculate conception of Mary also could be read into sūra 3,31/36: 'I seek refuge with thee for her and her progeny from Satan the stoned.' And the deeps of forced exegesis must have been reached in the notion that Mary's repairing 'to a height' (23,52/50) indicated the hill of the Assumption of Mary! But it has been questioned whether the Qur'ān does plainly teach a virginal conception of Jesus without a human father. Some modern Muslims and Christians, doubting the virgin birth on scientific or historical grounds, have sought to give a more natural interpretation to the words of both the Qur'ān and the Bible.

The old commentators considered that Jesus was 'born without a father'. Baiḍāwī thought that the angels addressing Mary were a spontaneous miracle in her honour, though he admitted that there were even then some who denied the doctrine of spontaneous miracles and others who said the angels had put the words into her thoughts.

Although the virgin birth was accepted that was not taken to give Jesus primacy over all other prophets, for such eminence would not depend upon the manner of his birth alone. Zwemer quoted modern Muslim teachers who said that 'the fact of the virgin birth does not necessarily prove the superiority of Jesus because "Adam had neither father nor mother, and was in this respect superior to Jesus" '.[1] Ibn Isḥāq suggests that this was already a point in the discussion in the Prophet's time with the Christians of Najrān and Abyssinia. 'Jesus was one who was formed in the womb – they do not attempt to deny that – like every other child of Adam . . . God created him by his spirit and his breathing . . . If they say, Jesus was created without a male (intervening), I created Adam from earth by that same power without a male or a female. And he was as Jesus was: flesh and blood and hair and skin. The creation of Jesus without a male is no more wonderful than this.'[2]

Some modern Muslim writers deny that the Qur'ān teaches the virgin birth. Such are: Sayyid Aḥmad Khān, Tawfīq Ṣidqī, Parwez, and Muḥammad 'Alī. Others, like Maulana Āzād, despite some rationalization, think that bearing in mind the context 'One must acknowledge without hesitation that the Qur'ān accepts the dogma'.[3] Aḥmad Khān comments that the statement that 'Mary guarded her chastity' does not mean that she never had intercourse with any man, but 'it means that she only had intercourse with her husband'. He and others proceed to interpret the story in a natural manner throughout. Mary's mother prayed for her, having 'in mind the time when Mary would be married and become a mother'. The mention of the

[1] *The Moslem Christ*, 1912, p. 116. [2] *The Life of Muhammad*, pp. 272, 276, 657.
[3] *Modern Muslim Koran Interpretation*, p. 70f.

choice by pens 'is the incident of her espousal', and the Gospel is referred to for confirmation that the Annunciation came to Mary after her espousal to Joseph (Lk. 1,27). M. 'Alī interprets Ibn Isḥāq's saying that Jesus was formed in the womb like every other child of Adam, to mean that 'Jesus was conceived by a woman in the manner in which all women conceive. Then she was delivered of him as women are delivered of their children.' So the conclusion is reached that Jesus was the legitimate child of Joseph and Mary, as against Jewish slanders of illegitimacy.[1]

Some modern Christian commentators interpret the Gospel narratives in similar fashion. It has been remarked that the Quranic story of the annunciation is much closer to Luke, who is concerned with Mary, than to Matthew who tells the story from Joseph's point of view. Much of the Lukan story has little hint of a virgin birth. 'The only words in this Gospel which involve the idea of conception without a human father are the patent interpolation of the evangelist at 3,23, and the two verses 34 and 35 in this section' [ch. 1].[2] The Magnificat is no doubt a later hymn, whether attributed either to Mary or Elizabeth, but it has no mention of an unusual birth. The story of the birth of Jesus in Luke 2 need not imply it, and at the presentation of the child Jesus in the temple there is reference several times to 'the child's father and mother' and to 'his parents'. Because of this some commentators consider that behind the present text of Luke was 'an earlier and unrecoverable form of the Annunciation in which Jesus was assumed to be the son of Joseph'. Hence the hints that Joseph was the parent. 'So far as we know the idea of conception without a human father was unknown in orthodox Judaism. But it was widely prevalent in the ancient world ... Thus when the Church moved out into the Hellenistic world of Caesarea, Antioch and beyond, it would be very natural that cognate ideas concerning the manner of the conception of Jesus should find a lodgement.'[3]

But the narrative of the annunciation itself is said to be not without difficulties in Luke. Mary is already betrothed to

[1] J. M. S. Baljon, *The Reforms and Religious Ideas of Sir Sayyid Aḥmad Khān*, 1949, pp. 82f.; 'Alī, *Holy Qur'ān*, pp. 141f., 597.
[2] J. M. Creed, *The Gospel according to St Luke*, 1930, p. 13.
[3] *ibid.*, pp. 14f.

Joseph. Why then is she troubled at the angel's message? For the words 'you shall conceive and bear a son' do not themselves 'raise the idea of conception *before marriage*, or of themselves imply *immediate* conception'.[1] A common Roman Catholic explanation is that this meant that Mary would always remain a virgin. But in that case it is asked why God had allowed her to become betrothed to Joseph? More forcible is the objection that Jesus is later called Mary's 'firstborn' (Luke 2,7). 'Brothers and sisters' of Jesus are named in Mark's Gospel, and there is no hint that these are other than the children of Joseph and Mary.

The story in Matthew is more plainly that of a virgin birth, though there is the genealogy which traces the descent of Jesus from Abraham and David through Joseph, which would seem pointless if Jesus were not Joseph's son.

Some early Christians appear to have had difficulty with the story of the virgin birth. The Jewish-Christian sect of Ebionites ('poor') said 'that Jesus was begotten of the seed of a man, and was chosen; and so by the choice of God he was called the Son of God from the Christ that came into him from above in the likeness of a dove. And they deny that he was begotten of God the Father, but say that he was created as one of the archangels, yet greater.' Apparently the early apocryphal Gospel according to the Hebrews attributed words to Jesus in which he spoke of 'my mother the Holy Spirit'. And Marcion of Pontus is said to have removed from the Gospel 'all that refers to the generation of the Lord'. But these are slight traces, and the apocryphal gospels delighted to add all manner of details to the comparatively restrained Gospel accounts. The Book of James already portrayed Joseph as an old man, who found a cave for Mary at the nativity, and sought out a midwife, Salome, who proved that Mary was still a virgin after the birth of the child.[2]

Whether the whole Quranic narrative can be interpreted of a natural or a virgin birth will continue to be debated. Two further points may be mentioned. The first is the close affinity

[1] Creed, p. 19.

[2] *Apocryphal New Testament*, pp. 2, 10, etc.; H. M. Gwatkin, *Selections from Early Christian Writers*, 1937 edn., p. 99. In the Acts of Thomas Jesus is called 'son of Joseph the carpenter.'

between the words spoken at the annunciation of the birth of John (Yaḥyā) and that of Jesus. This appears both in sūra 19 and in sūra 3. In 19,9–10 Zachariah inquires 'how shall I have a boy . . . seeing I have reached an advanced age', and is told 'So shall it be . . . it is easy for me'. The same is said in 19,20–21 to Mary when she asks 'How shall I have a boy, seeing that man hath not touched me?' and she is told, 'So shall it be . . . it is easy for me.' Similarly in 3,35/40 Zachariah is told in reply to his objection, 'So (shall it be), God doeth as he willeth'. And in 3,42/47 Mary also is told in response to her query, 'So (shall it be), God createth what he willeth, when he decideth upon a thing, he simply saith "Be!" and it is'. There is no suggestion that John was born without a human father, or by a miracle dispensing with the normal channels of human generation and birth, and so it is claimed by some modern commentators that the same applied to Jesus.

The second point is that the Qur'ān again and again denies that God begets or takes to himself offspring. One of the favourite sūras is 112, 'He brought not forth, nor hath he been brought forth'. And many times we read, God 'hath not taken to himself offspring', and 'far be it from him to have a son'. (25,2; 4,169/171; etc., etc.) The bearing of these statements upon the Christian use of the word 'Son' for Jesus will be discussed in a later chapter. Here it must be noted that the Qur'ān is strongly opposed to the notion of physical begetting by God. No doubt this was in opposition to the pagan attribution of wives and children to their gods. Al-Lāt, al-'Uzzā and Manāt, three of the principal goddesses of pre-Islamic Mecca, were said to be called daughters of God. So sūra 53,21 asks about them, 'have ye male issue and He female?' (See pp. 126–7.)

A similar objection against physical begetting of Christ may be reflected in the Book of James. Mary said to herself, 'Shall I verily conceive of the living God, and bring forth after the manner of all women?' And the angel replied, 'Not so, Mary, for a *power* of the Lord shall overshadow thee; wherefore also that holy thing which shall be born of thee shall be called the Son of the Highest'.[1] The word Son is used, in a technical

[1] *The Apocryphal New Testament*, p. 43.

sense, but the passage seems to show that there is no seed planted in the woman from above, but rather that the power of God overshadows her, or the Word decrees it. So too the Qur'ān simply declares the divine decree, the word 'Be', without saying whether the birth is to be by normal channels.

8

The Birth of Jesus

Sūra 19 proceeds with an account of the nativity or birth of Jesus:

19,22: 'So she bore [or 'conceived'] him, and withdrew with him to a place far away.

19,23: 'The birth-pangs drove her to the trunk of the palm-tree; she said: "Would that I had died before this, and become a forgetting, forgotten".

19,24: 'Then he called to her from beneath her [or 'the one that was below her called to her']: "Grieve not; thy Lord hath placed beneath thee a streamlet;

19,25: ' "Shake towards thee the trunk of the palm-tree, and it will let fall upon thee juicy [fruit, or 'dates'], ripe.

19,26: ' "So eat and drink and be of good cheer; and if thou see of mankind any one,

19,27/26: ' "Say: 'Verily I have vowed to the Merciful [al-Raḥmān] a fast, and I shall not speak today to one of human kind' ".

19,28/27: 'Then she brought him to her people, carrying him; they said: "O Mary, thou hast committed a thing improper;

19,29/28: ' "O daughter [lit. 'sister'] of Aaron, thy father was not a bad man nor was thy mother a harlot [or 'unchaste']".

19,30/29: 'Then she referred (them) to him; they said: "How shall we speak to one who is in the cradle, a child?"

19,31/30: 'He said: "Lo, I am the servant of God; he hath bestowed on me the Book, and hath made me a prophet;

19,32/31: 'And hath blessed me wherever I am, and hath

charged me with the Prayer and the Almsgiving as long as I live.' (*zakāt*, alms, used here in conjunction with *ṣalāt*, the ritual prayer, is perhaps used more technically than of Yaḥyā in 19,14, though the two stories have a number of parallels)

19,33/32: ' "And dutiful towards my mother, nor hath he made me a tyrant, wretched.

19,34/33: ' "And peace is upon me the day of my birth, and the day of my death, and the day of my being raised up alive".'

With this passage should be compared 23,52/50: 'We made them repair to a height with a secure abode and a spring'. Also there is 3,41/46: 'He will speak to the people in the cradle and as grown man.'

There are some links here with the canonical Gospels, though perhaps more with the apocryphal. The withdrawal 'to a place far away' has been taken to refer to Mary's journey from Nazareth to Bethlehem, which was a town though the child was placed 'in a manger'. A modern Muslim commentator says, 'the annunciation and the conception, we may suppose, took place in Bethlehem. It was a remote place, not only with reference to the distance of 71 miles from Nazareth, but because in Bethlehem itself the birth was in an obscure corner under a palm-tree, from which perhaps the babe was afterwards removed to a manger in a stable.[1]

Some writers have seen in the 'height with a secure abode [or 'a hollow'] and a spring' one of the places on the road during the flight of the parents of Jesus with their child into Egypt. Another Muslim tradition has placed Mary's tree on a hill near Damascus. The story of Hagar and Ishmael also comes to mind. Mary's agonized cries are quite natural, though some early Muslim mystics made curious meditations on Mary's 'mortal trouble' before abandoning herself to God again as she had done previously.[2]

The meaning of 'he called to her from beneath her' has been disputed and the reading is uncertain. Some have taken it to be an angelic voice, as in the Hagar story, probably the angel

[1] Yusuf 'Alī, commentary on the Qur'ān, p. 772.

[2] L. Massignon, *Essai sur les origines du lexique technique de la mystique musulmane*, 1954, p. 142n.

Gabriel, standing at the foot of the hill, while others thought it to be the baby Jesus. Some exegetes thought that Jesus spoke to his mother before birth, and assumed that the word 'beneath' here could not have its usual Arabic meaning and must be a foreign word meaning 'womb'.[1]

In the Gospel of Pseudo-Matthew, a Latin writing perhaps compiled about the eighth century though including older material, it is said that during the flight into Egypt Mary sat under a palm tree and wished for some of its fruit. Joseph was more worried about the lack of water. Jesus, sitting in Mary's lap, told the tree to bend down and give his mother some of its fruit, and it obeyed. Then he told it to rise up and give some of the water hidden under its roots, and a spring came out from which they drank and rejoiced. The Arabic Infancy Gospel says that they rested under a sycamore tree at Matarieh, and there Jesus made a spring gush out in which Mary washed his coat.[2] The sycamore at Matarieh, Heliopolis, is one of the four sites of the Flight venerated in Egypt by Christians and Muslims, and which it is said make Egypt a land of peace; but the present sycamore replaced in the seventeenth century an earlier palm tree, which in its turn no doubt stood for an ancient sacred tree. Ṭabarī said that Mary's tree was a dried up palm tree whose leaves had fallen and branches broken. He said that others maintained that in the temple there was a pillar of a palm tree which supported the building and that Mary leaned on this pillar, but he holds that the other story according to which Mary gave birth outside the town is more conformable to the Qur'ān. E. F. F. Bishop suggests that the 'streamlet' or 'rivulet' was Pilate's aqueduct at Bethlehem.[3]

Mary is told to vow a fast to the Merciful, al-Raḥmān, one of the favourite Quranic names for God and apparently pre-Islamic, possibly Christian, but incorporated into the new faith and occurring fifty-six times in the Qur'ān in addition to its use in the Bismillāh superscription of every sūra but one. This may be compared with the phrase in Mary's song, the Magnificat,

[1] *Foreign Vocabulary of the Qur'ān*, p. 32.
[2] P. Peeters, *Evangiles apocryphes*, ii, p. 24; *Apocryphal New Testament*, p. 75.
[3] In *The Muslim World*, lii, pp. 189ff.

'God my Saviour'. (Lk. 1,47) Commentators explain that the 'fast' means that she was to decline human conversation for a time on the plea of a vow to God. It does not mean abstinence from all food and drink, since Mary had just been told to eat dates and drink from the stream. This is the only mention of fasting in the Meccan suras.

When Mary returned home with the baby she was accused of immorality. This may be compared with Joseph's hesitation, 'not willing to make her a public example, he was minded to put her away privately', till the angel reassured him. (Matt. 1,19) There has been discussion over the phrase, 'sister of Aaron' (*ukht Hārūn*). Some take it as 'descendant' of Aaron, since *ukht* is not limited to close blood relationship and Mary was of Levitical race. Others take it as a sign of confusion with the Miriam who was sister of Aaron. Yet others regard it as a *kunya*, a surname or epithet from Mary's famous ancestor Miriam.

The child speaking 'in the cradle' is mentioned in 3,41/46; 5,109/110; and 19,30/29. The traditions and older commentators took this literally. Baiḍāwī said that both as an infant and as a grown man Jesus spoke in the language of the prophets without variation. He even added that it was said that Mary also when small spoke as Jesus did later. Another tradition said that eleven children had spoken in their cradles, though a contradictory comment was that Jesus was the only one to do this, since he was the Mahdī, 'the guided one', who had spoken from the cradle (*mahd*).[1]

Ibn Isḥāq said that the Christians from Najrān who came to see Muḥammad argued that Jesus 'spoke from the cradle and this is something that no child of Adam has ever done'.[2] The only apocryphal reference seems to be the scribal note at the beginning of the Arabic Infancy Gospel, saying that 'Jesus spoke, being in the cradle, and said to his mother, "I am Jesus, the Son of God, the Word, which you have borne as the angel Gabriel announced to you" '. The modern editor remarks that this anecdote must have been current fairly early among Arab Christians.[3]

[1] See *Jésus selon le Coran*, p. 25n.
[2] *Life of Muhammad*, p. 271.
[3] *Evangiles apocryphes*, ii, p. 1.

Modern commentators, however, tend to interpret this saying as applying to Jesus at a later age, though still in his minority. It is said that old and learned Jews would speak of a boy as a mere child in the cradle and would disdain to address one so young. Yusuf 'Alī tries to have it both ways, saying that the child Jesus spoke by a miracle, defended his mother, and preached to an unbelieving audience; then he quotes the Gospel sayings that the child Jesus advanced in wisdom and in favour with God and men and disputed with the doctors in the temple. No doubt the most satisfactory parallel is the Gospel story of the boy Jesus going with his parents to Jerusalem, asking questions of the learned, and saying, 'Did you not know that I was bound to be in my Father's house?' (Lk. 2,49) The Gospel says that Jesus was then twelve years of age, and he would still be a minor. At the age of thirteen a Jewish boy attains his religious majority and becomes a 'son of the commandment' (*bar mitzvah*), thenceforward able to chant the law and read the lesson in the synagogue service.

It has been debated whether the Qur'ān teaches that the birth, as distinct from the conception, of Jesus was miraculous. There is no suggestion that Mary's pangs were abnormal, and no legendary story of a midwife to prove her continued virginal state such as some of the apocrypha related. A Muslim commentator says that 'an opinion which seems to be more popular than theological, and which is felt rather than explicit amongst Muslims, sees the birth as happening in the ordinary way'. It is known that Spanish Muslims denied the perpetual virginity of Mary.[1]

This section of sūra 19 ends with these words:

19,35/34: 'That is Jesus, son of Mary, – a statement of the truth concerning which they are in doubt.

19,36/35: 'It is not for God to take to himself any offspring; glory be to him! when he decides upon a thing, he simply says: "Be!" and it is.

19,37/36: 'Verily God is my Lord and your Lord, so serve him; this is a straight path.

19,38/37: 'But the sects disagreed among themselves; so woe to

[1] See *Jésus selon le Coran*, p. 27.

those who have disbelieved because of the witnessing of a mighty day!'

The 'statement of truth' (or 'in word of truth', see earlier, p. 46) is to clear up the doubt about the purity of Mary and the birth of Jesus by divine command. God does not 'take to himself' or acquire offspring, in the manner of pagan deities. This statement may also contradict the Adoptionist heresy which held that Jesus had 'become' Son of God or was 'added' to the deity; this is a heresy to Christians as well as to Muslims. The phrase, 'God is my Lord and your Lord' recalls the Gospel word of Jesus, 'my God and your God'. (John 20,17) 'This is a straight path' is a common Quranic phrase, meaning this is plain teaching, a direct path, a narrow way.

'But the sects disagreed', and this was the tragedy of the early church, as well as the disbelief of the Jews. The Christians of the Byzantine rite who visited Muḥammad are said to have 'differed among themselves' concerning Jesus, 'saying he is God; and he is the Son of God; and he is the third person of the Trinity'.[1] But those who disbelieved will be proved wrong by the witness of the day of judgement. 4,157/159 says that 'on the day of resurrection, he [Jesus] will be regarding them a witness'.

The partly parallel account of the annunciation and birth of Jesus in sūra 3 concludes thus:

3,52/59: 'Jesus in God's eyes is in the same position as Adam', [or 'the likeness (*mathal*) of Jesus, in God's sight, is as Adam's likeness']; He created him of dust, then said to him "Be!" and he is.

3,53/60: 'The truth from thy Lord [or 'the truth is of God'], so be not of those who doubt!

3,54/61: 'If anyone dispute with thee concerning him after the knowledge which has come to thee, say: "Come, let us call our sons and your sons, our wives and your wives, ourselves and yourselves, then let us make earnest prayer and lay the curse of God upon those who lie".

3,55/62: 'This is certainly the true account; there is nothing of the nature of a god except God; God is the Sublime, the Wise.'

The birth of Jesus by divine decree is compared both with

[1] *Life of Muhammad*, p. 271.

that of John the Baptist and with that of Adam. Sura 38,72 says that Adam was made through the Spirit of God: 'I have formed him and breathed into him some of my spirit.' So Jesus is called 'a spirit from him'. (4,169/171)

Reference has been made to Ibn Isḥāq's account of the debate with the Najrān Christians in which it was said that if Jesus had no father Adam had neither father nor mother. This is the negative side. The positive side is firstly that both Jesus and Adam came by the will of God to do his service. Secondly Adam 'was as Jesus was: flesh and blood and hair and skin'.[1] This is important, because it stresses the true humanity of Jesus, which the church has sometimes neglected. So the Qur'ān said of Jesus and Mary, 'both of them ate food'. (5,79/75) This is in full accordance with the Gospel where it is said many times that Jesus ate and drank with publicans and sinners, with Pharisees and his disciples. Such a verse as John 4,32, 'I have food to eat of which you know nothing', had a purely spiritual reference. But later ages could obviously exaggerate this. In the apocryphal Gospels generally Jesus is shown as a human, though very precocious, child; the young prodigy sowed and reaped and threshed one corn of wheat in a day and fed all the poor of the village with it. Probably modern Christians, thanks to a century of Biblical criticism, have a better understanding of the humanity of Jesus than any generation since the first century.

The Bible makes a comparison of Jesus with Adam, by showing him as the Last Adam or Second Man. Paul stressed this in showing Adam as a figure or type of 'him that was to come', namely Jesus. 'The first man, Adam, became a living being, whereas the last Adam has become a life-giving spirit.' (Rom. 5,14; 1 Cor. 15,45f.) Some writers have worked out further parallels between the temptations of Jesus and that of Adam; the grasping of equality with God by Adam, and the renunciation of Jesus, but this is speculative.[2] A closer New Testament comparison is with the title 'Son of Man', which may both affirm the humanity and also the communal mission of Jesus.

In modern times some theologians, notably Emil Brunner,

[1] *Life of Muhammad*, p. 276.

[2] *The Names of Jesus*, p. 153.

have spoken of Jesus as the ideal Man, the archetype, the normal man, man as God intended him to be when he created him. Perhaps a fuller understanding of the significance of Christ is to be found along such lines. But there is still need to beware of the constant danger of Docetism, treating Jesus as if he were not fully human; he was a real man and not a type. The nature of Christ is seen not simply in his birth, but in his life, and not only in his words but in the grace and compassion of his living which revealed the nature of God as love.

9

Works of Jesus

THAT Jesus was a great healer of the sick is confirmed by the Qur'ān. His miracles are mentioned in summary form with little detail, that is, they are accepted but not recounted. Isḥāq Ḥusaini says, 'the Qur'ān enumerated the miracles of Christ which were signs of his prophecy . . . It is noteworthy that Muḥammad did not attribute miracles to himself. The Qur'ān is his only miracle . . . All these miracles Christ produced by the will of God in order to convince those who doubted his mission.'[1] The Gospel, which gives the detail of the miracles of Jesus, attributes them to his compassion for the needy.

5,109–110: 'God said: "O Jesus, son of Mary, remember my goodness to thee and to her who brought thee forth, when I supported thee by the Holy Spirit in speaking to the people in the cradle and as grown man; when I taught thee the Book and the Wisdom and the Torah and the Gospel; when thou wert creating figures like birds from clay by my permission, and then breathing upon them so that they became birds by my permission; when thou wert healing the blind and the leprous by my permission; when thou wert causing the dead to come forth by my permission; when I restrained the Children of Israel from thee, when thou didst come to them with the Evidences and those of them who had disbelieved said: 'This is nothing but magic clear' ".'

3,43/49: 'I have come to you with a sign from your Lord (to wit) that I shall create for you from clay the form of a bird and

[1] *Christ in the Qur'ān and in Modern Arabic Literature*, p. 3.

I shall breathe into it and it shall become a bird by the permission of God, and I shall heal the blind, and the leprous, and bring the dead to life by the permission of God, and I shall announce to you what ye may eat, and what ye may store in your houses; verily in that is a sign [*āya*] for you, if ye are believers.'

It has been common in modern times to distinguish between the 'healing miracles' of Jesus and the 'nature miracles'. The latter are such stories in the Gospel as stilling the storm, walking on the water, and changing water into wine. Some critics may take these as having a spiritual meaning, or they may be regarded as resting upon misunderstanding or the exaggeration of a later age. But that Jesus was a healer of the sick seems beyond dispute. The Qur'ān refers to the healings, and says nothing of the nature miracles mentioned in the Gospels.

The reference to clay birds flying away, however, may seem to come into the category of nature miracle. It does not come in the canonical Gospels, but appears in many of the apocrypha and lingers to this day in Christian legend. The Gospel of Thomas, which goes back at least to the sixth century, from whence there is a Syriac manuscript, says: 'This little child Jesus when he was five years old was playing at the ford of a brook . . . and having made soft clay, he fashioned thereof twelve sparrows. And it was the sabbath when he did these things . . . Jesus clapped his hands together and cried out to the sparrows and said to them: Go! and the sparrows took their flight and went away chirping.'[1]

This story also appears in the Jewish Toldoth Jeshu. Similarly in the Arabic Infancy Gospel Jesus is said to have made clay figures of animals, and made them walk and jump; he also made figures of birds and caused them to fly. Ibn Isḥāq said that the Christians of Najrān argued the divinity of Christ from his miracles, for he made 'clay birds and then breathed into them so that they flew away'.[2]

[1] *Apocryphal New Testament*, p. 49; H. J. Bardsley, *Reconstructions of Early Christian Documents*, I, p. 187.

[2] *Evangiles apocryphes*, ii, pp. 44f.; *Life of Muhammad*, p. 271.

Muslim commentators have traditionally accepted this story as a statement of fact. But modernist Muslim writers try to minimize miraculous elements in the Qur'ān as much as possible. M. 'Alī says that this story is perfectly intelligible if taken as a parable, but quite incomprehensible as a statement of fact. 'A prophet's dignity is much above such actions as the making of toy birds.' It might be replied that a really human child does not require dignity. But 'Alī interprets the word 'bird' (*ṭair*) as meaning a brave or spiritual man. What is meant here is that Jesus 'by breathing a spirit into mortals, will make them rise above those who are low upon the earth'. Sayyid Aḥmad Khān commented on the *fa* in *fa-yakūnu*, 'and it shall become' (3,43/49), that according to Arabic philologists 'the real happening of the thing cannot be accepted as long as no other proof is available. And so from the way in which the Koran relates this event it becomes clear that it did not actually take place, but that it was merely a fancy of Jesus when he played with other children.'[1] Few Christians nowadays believe in the story of clay birds flying and, if they used it at all, most would prefer whatever spiritual lesson might be extracted from it.

The Qur'ān says that Jesus healed the blind and the lepers and raised the dead to life. The abundant detail of these actions is found in the canonical Gospels. Traditional Muslim commentators have accepted them without difficulty. Baiḍāwī said that it was recorded that thousands used to gather to Jesus, those of them who were able came to him, while to those who were unable Jesus went himself. He said that Jesus healed by prayer only. As Muslim writers came into closer contact with Christians they assimilated stories from the Bible and from legend. So there are accounts of Jesus healing the sick, raising the dead, walking on the water, and making loaves appear out of the ground.

Some rationalist modern Muslim commentators try to find natural explanations for the healing miracles, as well as for others. Thus M. 'Alī says that 'the miracle of Jesus healing the sick has been rationally explained . . . All the stories of healing

[1] M. 'Alī, *Holy Qur'ān*, p. 144: J. M. S. Baljon, *Religious Ideas of Sir Sayyid Aḥmad Khān*, pp. 81f.

the sick have arisen from the spiritual healing of the sick.'[1] He quotes in support of this view the Biblical commentator T. K. Cheyne who wrote in 1903. But this sceptical attitude towards the possibility of healing the body by spiritual means is much less acceptable today than it was at the beginning of the century, owing to the great development of psychotherapy in modern times. Even by 1922 a study called *Miracles and the New Psychology* was able to declare that in the Gospels 'the particulars of the miracles of healing upon which most reliance can be placed are not themselves incompatible with the view that such healing was accomplished through the agency of ascertainable psychological laws'.[2] In other words, the healing miracles of Jesus were not merely of the spirit, but were of both soul and body. Modern study increases still more the understanding of the health or disease-provoking effect of the mind upon the body.

Jesus is also said to have raised the dead, but no details are given in the Qur'ān. In the Gospels the three cases related are those of the daughter of Jairus, the widow's son at Nain, and Lazarus. (Mk. 5; Lk. 7; Jn. 11) Dr. L. D. Weatherhead has pointed out that these all seem to have been young people, and so perhaps more responsive to psychic influences than adults; though whether all were truly dead, at least the first two, cannot be decisively established. M. 'Alī interprets the Quranic reference as meaning that Jesus 'quickened to life those who are spiritually dead'.[3]

A further well-known Quranic story that may seem to be miraculous is in sūra 5, commonly called The Table:

5,112–114: 'The apostles said: "O Jesus, son of Mary, is thy Lord able to send down to us a table from heaven?" He replied: "Show piety towards God, if ye are believers". They said: "Our desire is that we may eat from it and our hearts be at peace, that we may know that thou hast spoken truthfully to us and that to it we may be among the witnesses". Jesus, son of Mary, said: "O God our Lord, send down to us a table from heaven, to be to us a festival, to the first and to the last of us, and a sign [*āya*] from thee, and do thou provide

[1] *Holy Qur'ān*, p. 145.   [2] by E. R. Micklem, p. 130.
[3] 'Alī, p. 145; L. D. Weatherhead, *Psychology, Religion and Healing*, 2nd edn., 1963.

for us, for thou art the best of providers". God said: "Verily I am going to send it down to you; so if any of you afterwards disbelieve, I shall assuredly punish them as I punish no one else of (all) the worlds".'

It is not clear whether this parallels the Gospel story of the Last Supper or the Feeding of the Five Thousand. (Mk. 6,34ff.; 14,12ff.) Some writers have referred it to the prayer which Jesus taught his disciples, 'Give us this day our daily bread'. (Matt. 6,11) But sura 5,114 says that this 'is to be to us a festival'. The word *'īd* is used which is applied also to Muslim festivals, and so this would be appropriate for the Christian Eucharist or Lord's Supper, which Christians have celebrated as their chief ritual. Hence some Muslim writers said that the table or food came on a Sunday.

Some of the commentators and later versions, however, seemed to assimilate this narrative to the Feeding of the Five Thousand and this has affected Islamic tradition. Baiḍāwī said that it was narrated how a red table of food (*sufrah*) was sent down upon two clouds, as the disciples watched, until it was right in their midst. There was cooked fish without scales and fins and very greasy. Salt was at the head and vinegar at the tail and around all kinds of herbs except leeks. There were also five loaves. This garnishing of the fish may be purely imaginary, but it is tempting to see in it a reference to the various herbs used in the Jewish Passover *seder*. In the oldest Coptic church in Egypt, Abū Sarga or St. Sergius in Cairo, are ancient paintings of the Last Supper showing vegetables on the table as well as loaves of bread and bottles of wine.

The five loaves, however, bring us back to the Feeding of the Five Thousand. Baiḍāwī said that Simon asked, 'O Spirit of God, is this the food of this world or the food from heaven?' Jesus replied, 'It is not from hence. God, to whom be praise and honour, has brought it into being by his power.' This may be compared with the Gospel saying of Jesus, 'it was not Moses that gave you the bread out of heaven; but my Father giveth you the true bread out of heaven. For the bread of God is that which cometh down out of heaven and giveth life unto the world'. (John 6,32f.)

Some of the popular Muslim stories take the table to have come down literally and visibly from the sky, and Ṭabarī said that according to one version it stayed with Jesus and his disciples for three days and then was taken up to heaven again. But in another version, he says, there was no table from heaven but Jesus multiplied the bread, and he recounts the story of the Feeding of the Five Thousand. Yet others, he said, declare that Jesus prayed and his disciples said, 'We have no need of a table, for we are believers and faithful to our belief'. For some Ṣūfī mystics the table was a symbol of the truths of mystical knowledge, the nourishment of the spirit.

Most modern commentators reject the notion of a 'red tray' sent down physically from heaven. Maulana Āzād remarked that the apostles had food with them (in the Five Thousand story) but no table or tray was available, and so they asked if Jesus could not pray to God to provide a table from heaven. Jesus told them to fear God and make no such requests, and it is not actually said in the Qur'ān that God did send the table down. M. 'Alī gives an interpretation of the word 'table' (*mā'ida*) as meaning also 'a table with food on it', and so just 'food'. Hence Jesus gives food, heavenly food, which is for the heart and is spiritual knowledge. But Jeffery suggests that *mā'ida*, which is a late word and occurs only in this Medinan verse, may come from an Ethiopic word which among Abyssinian Christians is used almost technically for the Lord's Table, i.e. the Last Supper.[1]

In an interesting recent discussion of the Qur'ān and the Last Supper it has been pointed out that at the Feeding of the Five Thousand the disciples 'in no way requested "a table from heaven"'. But at the Last Supper 'the disciples did initiate their enquiry as to where the Passover should be prepared'. Hence, though the Quranic passage could be thought to fit another setting also, it does bear several features that have very close kinship to the 'table' in the Upper Room. 'The "table" is said by Jesus to constitute a festival from the beginning to the end of Christian history ("to the first and to the last of us",

[1] *Modern Muslim Koran Interpretation*, p. 24; M. 'Alī, p. 274; *Foreign Vocabulary of the Qur'ān*, p. 255.

5,114), and it is said further to be a "sign", or (in the loose sense) sacrament, from God.' But there was no perpetuity or repetitition about the occasions of public feeding in the Gospel. Deeper than this aspect, however, says this writer, is the fact that in sura 5 the 'heavenly board' has a status as a returning 'festival', and so in some sense a memorial, and that it is linked with the basic Quranic concept of divine 'signs'. The Quranic situation does not exclude, but rather requires 'a set of circumstances in which the memorial "table" would be likely ... Jesus' table, being a returning festival for the whole sequence of disciples, would be a "sign from God" and a nourishing'. This is said to require an investigation of the Qur'ān's involvement in the sacramental realm and in the Crucifixion, which will be considered later.[1]

It is interesting that early Christians assimilated the Feeding of the Five Thousand to the Last Supper. In the catacombs in Rome early paintings depict the table of the Eucharist, with twelve baskets for the fragments of the Feeding in front of it.

Modern scholars differ as to whether the Gospel story of the Feeding of the Five Thousand is to be regarded as a miracle or not. 'If a miraculous interpretation has been superimposed, it happened before Mark was written.' But whether it was meant to suggest a multiplication of five loaves and two fishes or not, it is clear that the story was treasured long after the event on which it was based, because of 'its symbolic relevance to the Eucharist', which was the Christian 'festival' above all others.[2]

It is curious that the Gospel according to John, which gives the Feeding and a long discussion of its inner meaning, omits the institution of the Eucharist at the Last Supper, as if enough had already been said. This Gospel denies that manna or any other material food really came down from heaven. God alone gives the true heavenly bread which gives life to the world. (Jn. 6,31ff.)

Several times in the Qur'ān Jesus is said to have been given

[1] 'Abd al-Tafāhum, 'The Qur'ān and the Holy Communion', in *The Muslim World*, 1959, pp. 239ff.

[2] V. Taylor, *The Gospel according to St Mark*, p. 321.

the 'evidences' or 'clear signs' (*bayyināt*), and to have come with them to men. (2,81/87; 2,254/253; 5,110; 43,63; 61,6) Sometimes men rejected them as 'magic manifest'. (5,110; 61,6) Some translators have rendered 'evidences' as 'evident miracles', and this may seem reasonable in some contexts. The scribes from Jerusalem rejected the miracles of Jesus, and the Gospel reports that they declared him to be casting out demons 'by the prince of the demons'. (Mk. 3,22)

But other prophets are also said in the Qur'ān to have come with the 'evidences', for example Moses in 2,86/92, And Muḥammad is assured of the 'evidences', which are the verses of the Qur'ān (2,93/99; 98,1; etc.) Elsewhere the Prophet was told to refuse to give any other sign, for he was 'but a human being sent as a messenger', while the Qur'ān was 'healing and mercy'. (17,95/93) Similarly in the Gospel Jesus refused to work signs to prove his mission, 'there shall be no sign given to this generation'. (Mk. 8,12) The healing miracles of Jesus came from his being moved with compassion at the cries and faith of the sick, but he preferred men to believe through his teaching.

The Evidences of Jesus, then, are his teachings as well as his miracles, in the prophetic succession. This is made clear in 43,63: 'When Jesus came with the Evidences, he said: "I have come to you with Wisdom, and in order to make clear to you some of that in which ye differ".'

The Evidence that Jesus had was the Gospel (Injīl), which he was taught by God. So says 5,110: 'I taught thee the Book and the Wisdom and the Torah and the Gospel . . . when thou didst come to them with the Evidences'. The Gospel 'contains guidance and light, confirming the Torah which was before it, and as guidance and admonition to those who show piety'. (5,50/46) The revelation of God is said to be continuous, from Law to Gospel to Qur'ān. The verses that follow the last quotation go on to say to Muḥammad, 'to thee also have we sent down the Book with the Truth, confirming the Book which was before it'.

The mission of Jesus, in the Qur'ān, is that of bringing the Good News (Injīl), confirming the Torah, showing the Wisdom and Evidences of God, teaching prayer and almsgiving, and being a sign, a mercy, an example, and a witness. With those who follow Jesus truly God 'made a covenant', they are 'above the unbelievers', and he will reward them on the day of resurrection. (3,48/55; 5,17/14)

10

Words of Jesus

(a) Sayings

THE teachings of Jesus are in the Gospel, and the Qur'ān does not repeat them. The Qur'ān simply says that the Good News (Injīl) given to Jesus confirms the Torah and gives 'guidance and light'. Ṭabarī said that some laws which were forbidden by the Torah were allowed by the Gospel, and when Muḥammad came he also allowed that which was permitted by the Gospel.

Some actual words are attributed to Jesus in the Qur'ān, however, while there are other sayings that recall verses of the Gospel. The former will be considered first briefly:

3,43f./40f. [Jesus said]: 'I have come to you with a sign from your Lord (to wit) that I shall create for you from clay the form of a bird and I shall breathe into it and it will become a bird by the permission of God, and I shall heal the blind and the leprous, and bring the dead to life by the permission of God, and I shall announce to you what ye may eat, and what ye may store up in your houses; verily in that is a sign for you if ye are believers. Confirming what is before me of the Torah, and that I may make allowable for you some things which have been forbidden to you; I have brought you a sign from your Lord, so act piously towards God and obey me. Verily God is my Lord and your Lord, so serve him, this is a straight path.'

The first part of this saying has been referred to in the previous chapter. Some of it closely resembles the message sent by Jesus through disciples of John the Baptist: 'the blind receive their sight, the lepers are cleansed, the dead are raised up'. (Matt. 11,5) There are also several sayings of Jesus about eating, fasting, storing up and worrying. (Matt. 6,16–26) The attitude of Jesus to the Law, and relaxation of its rigidity, is expressed at the beginning of his famous sermon. (Matt. 5,17ff.) Baiḍāwī said that this shows that the code of Jesus supersedes that of Moses.

The phrase 'God is my Lord' will be mentioned again below. The 'straight path' is like the 'straitened way'. (Matt. 7,14)

3,45f./52f.: 'So when Jesus perceived unbelief on their part he said "Who are my helpers [*anṣār*] towards God?" The apostles replied: "We are the helpers of God, we have believed in God, do thou testify that we are submitting ones [Muslims]. O our Lord, we believe in what thou hast sent down and followed the messenger [*rasūl*]: so write us down among the witnesses".'

This passage recalls the question of Jesus to the disciples in the Gospel: 'Would you also go away?' Simon Peter answered him: 'Lord, to whom should we go? thou hast the words of eternal life. And we have believed and know that thou art the holy one of God'. Ibn Isḥāq several times attributes to Muḥammad the words: 'Do not hang back from me as the disciples hung back from Jesus, son of Mary . . . and Jesus complained of them to God'.

The word used for 'apostles' or disciples of Jesus is *ḥawārī* (pl. *ḥawārīyūn*) which Baiḍāwī and others took to come from the Arabic 'he who wears white clothes', and they said that the followers of Jesus were so named owing to the purity of their minds and the holiness of their thoughts. But modern scholars find little doubt that the word is a borrowing from Ethiopic. It is used only of disciples of Jesus and in late Medinan passages, and may have been taken over from the emigrants who returned from Abyssinia. However, Jeffery thinks it very possible that the word was already current in Arabia.[1] Soon Muslim tradition said that the twelve Medinans who made a covenant with Muḥammad were 'just as the apostles' of Jesus, and were called *ḥawārīyūn* like them.

[1] *Foreign Vocabulary of the Qur'ān*, pp. 115f.; and *Encyclopaedia of Islam*, art. *Ḥawārī*.

The disciples of Jesus are also called 'helpers' (*anṣār*), which was the honourable name given to the 'helpers' of Medina who supported Muḥammad. This word may also be linked with the other Quranic word for Christians, Naṣārā; see the later chapter on the Christians.

Practically the same words as 3,45/52 are found in sura 61,14: 'Jesus, son of Mary, said to the apostles: "Who are my helpers towards God?" and the apostles said: "We are the helpers of God".'

Further sayings are in sura 5:

5,112: 'When the apostles said: "O Jesus, son of Mary, is thy Lord able to send down to us a table from heaven?" He replied: "Show piety towards God, if ye are believers".'

5,114: 'Jesus, son of Mary, said: "O God our Lord, send down to us a table from heaven, to be to us a festival, to the first and to the last of us, and a sign from thee, and do thou provide for us, for thou art the best of providers".'

These verses have already been considered in the previous chapter. The closest Gospel parallels are in John 6, with the questions of the disciples first, the giving thanks to God, the connexion with the Passover festival, but with this feeding as the true bread of heaven.

5,116–118 recalls God's questions whether Jesus had taught that he and his mother should be taken as two gods apart from God, and it continues: 'He [Jesus] replied: "Glory be to thee! it is not for me to say what to me is not true [or 'what I have no right to say'); if I did say it, thou knowest it; thou knowest what is in my (inner) self ['soul', *nafs*], but I know not what is in thy (inner) self; verily it is thou who art the knower of secret [or 'unseen'] things. I did not say anything to them but what thou didst command me: 'Serve God, my Lord and your Lord'; I was a witness over them as long as I remained amongst them, but when thou didst take me to thyself, it was thou who wert the watcher over them, for thou over everything art witness. If thou dost punish them – well, they are thy servants; if thou dost forgive them – well, thou art the Sublime, the Wise".'

A similar saying had occurred earlier in this same sūra,

5,76/72: 'the Messiah said: "O children of Israel, serve God my Lord and your Lord" '.

Several times the phrase 'my Lord and your Lord' is repeated, and it recalls at once the word of Jesus in the Gospel, 'my God and your God'. (John 20,17) Also from this same Gospel come closely similar words to 5,117, in the prayer of Jesus to God: 'While I was with them I kept them in thy name . . . but now I come to thee . . . keep them in thy name . . . sanctify them in the truth . . . that they may be perfected into one; that the world may believe.' (John 17, 12ff.) It is interesting that there are particularly close parallels between the Quranic passages and the Gospel according to John. A similar exhortation to Christian unity as in the Johannine passage is in sura 42,11/13: 'What we laid as a charge upon Abraham and Moses and Jesus, saying: "Establish the religion and do not divide into parties regarding it" .'

Sūra 19,31–34 has already been discussed in connexion with the birth stories, but it may be repeated here for completeness: 'He [Jesus] said: "Lo, I am the servant of God; he hath
> bestowed on me the Book, and hath made me a prophet; and hath made me blessed wherever I am, and hath charged me with the Prayer and the Almsgiving as long as I live: and dutiful towards my mother, nor hath he made me a tyrant, wretched. And peace is upon me the day of my birth, and the day of my death, and the day of my being raised up alive".'

That Jesus may have seen himself as the Suffering Servant of Isaiah 53 was suggested in chapter 4. It may appear from Mark 1,11 onwards, and the early church soon applied to Jesus the prophecies of the Servant of God. Jesus came proclaiming the kingdom of God and calling men to believe in the Gospel. (Mark 1,15) In Luke 4 he took the book, read of the prophecy fulfilled, and announced good tidings to the poor and sick. His teaching on prayer and almsgiving is in his Sermon. (Matt. 6) His duty to his mother is expressed in Luke 2,51, and other places right up to the end. (John 19,25f.) His death and rising again are spoken of several times in the Gospel before the event. (Mark 8,31f., etc.)

Sūra 43,63–64 says: 'When Jesus came with the Evidences,

he said: "I have come to you with Wisdom, and in order to make clear to you some of that in which ye differ; so show piety towards God and obey me. Lo, God is my Lord and your Lord, so serve him; this is a straight path".'

The Gospel shows Jesus pointing the way between the old debates about the Law and its prescriptions. (Matt. 5,17f.; Mark 12,13ff.) He is filled with Wisdom (*sophia*, for Hebrew *hokmah*, like Arabic *ḥikma*), and indeed he is a child of wisdom. (Matt. 11,19) Jesus constantly called men to follow him and worship God, 'my God and your God'. This is the narrow and straight way. (John 20,17; Matt. 7,13f.)

Sūra 48,29 has a direct reference to the Gospel. Speaking of believers, it says: 'What they are compared to ['their likeness', *mathal*] in the Gospel is a seed which puts forth its shoot and strengthens it, so that it grows stout and straight upon its stalk, to the admiration of the sowers.' In the Gospel Jesus spoke of the seed which springs up and grows, first the blade, then the ear, then the full corn in the ear, and when the fruit is ripe the sower puts in the sickle. Or again, the grain of mustard seed grows up and becomes greater than all plants, so that birds can settle in its shade. (Mark 4,26f., 30f.)

(b) *aḥmadu*

Considerable discussion has ranged around the interpretation of sūra 61,6 which Bell translates: 'Jesus, son of Mary, said: "O children of Israel, I am God's messenger to you, confirming the Torah which was before me, and announcing the good tidings of the messenger who will come after me, bearing the name Aḥmad.'

This is the last and most remarkable direct statement which the Qur'ān puts into the mouth of Jesus. But an interesting variant on this verse was given by one of Muḥammad's secretaries, Ubayy b. Ka'b, who rendered it: 'O children of Israel, I am God's messenger to you, and I announce to you a prophet whose community will be the last community and by which God will put the seal on the prophets and messengers.' It may be noted that this does not speak of Aḥmad, but it clearly refers to a prophet who will seal up prophets and messengers. However, the first version is the official one, and it has commonly been taken to mean that Aḥmad is Muḥammad, who was thus prophesied by Jesus.

Ibn Isḥāq, in his life of the Prophet, has similar but significantly different words, and these give a hint of another interpretation. 'Among the things which have reached me about what Jesus the son of Mary stated in the Gospel . . . is extracted from what John the Apostle set down for them . . . "When the Comforter has come whom God will send to you from the Lord's presence, and the spirit of truth which will have gone forth from the Lord's presence he (shall bear) witness of me and ye also, because ye have been with me from the beginning. I have spoken unto you about this that ye should not be in doubt".' Ibn Isḥāq then adds: 'The Munaḥḥemana (God bless and preserve him!) in Syriac is Muḥammad; in Greek he is the paraclete.'[1]

Two points may be noted at once. There is no mention of a name Aḥmad in this passage. Secondly, neither Ibn Isḥāq nor Ibn Hishām, who edited and enlarged the Life later, make any reference to sura 61. Both writers of course knew the Qur'ān well and they often quote it in appropriate contexts throughout the Life. 'The implication is that neither Ibn Hishām nor his predecessor knew anything about the surmised reading as Aḥmad. Their concern was not for any similarity in name.'[2]

Guillaume, in his translation of Ibn Isḥāq, notes that his quotation of the Gospel (John 15,23ff.) is taken from the Palestinian Syriac Lectionary and not from the ordinary Bible of the Syriac-speaking churches. The Palestinian lectionary renders 'Comforter', whereas all other Syriac versions render 'Paraclete' following the Greek. The Munaḥḥemana means 'life-giver', but in this context it must mean a consoler or comforter. Ibn Isḥāq's virtual identification of this name with Muḥammad is undoubtedly stretching resemblances rather far. More to the point is his reference to the coming of the Spirit of truth.

[1] *The Life of Muhammad*, pp. 103f.

[2] See articles by A. Guthrie and E. F. F. Bishop, *Muslim World*, xli, pp. 251ff., and L. Bevan Jones, *Moslem World*, x, pp. 112ff.

The word translated 'Comforter' or 'Advocate' in the Gospel is 'Paraclete' in Greek. It is used of the Holy Spirit in the Gospel, and of Jesus himself once in the epistles. (1 John 2,1) Paraclete was a difficult word to understand, and many versions transmitted the word without translating it. Thus in the Gospel in Syriac it is rendered *paraqleto*' and in Arabic *fāraqlīt*. It has often been suggested that *parakletos*, 'comforter', was confused with *periklutos*, 'celebrated'. Since 'celebrated' or 'praised' is the meaning of Aḥmad, commentators and editors have assumed that Aḥmad was predicted in the Gospel, by name. But it is hard to substantiate this. The new *Encyclopaedia of Islam* says that the adoption of *fāraqlīt* into Arabic from the Gospel was 'impossible' so early. 'The Muslims did indeed apply to Muḥammad the prediction of the Paraclete, before the middle of the second century A.H., but the terms used are either the Greek *parakletos* or its correct Aramaic translation menaḥḥemānā.'[1]

On the other hand some western commentators have suggested that the words 'whose name is Aḥmad' (*ismu-hu aḥmadu*) were interpolated into the Qur'ān to prove that Jesus prophesied the coming of Muḥammad by name. But if this were so it would be difficult to understand why the name Muḥammad had not been interpolated, since it was much more obvious. Why was the form not used by which his contemporaries knew him, and which occurs in a rather similar context in sūra 47,2? 'What has been sent down to Muḥammad.'

Was Aḥmad the Prophet's name? This has been assumed in later Islam, but it is not at all sure. Bukhārī records a tradition: 'I heard the Messenger of God say: "I have several names; I am Muḥammad, I am Aḥmad, I am al-Māḥi" '. This might suggest that there was doubt over his other names. Another tradition said that a voice told Amina, the mother of the Prophet, to call her son Aḥmad. But it is doubtful whether she did so, for the names are distinct, even though both come from the same root *ḥmd*. W. M. Watt, after a careful examination of the instances in which Aḥmad occurred concludes that 'Muslim children were practically never called Aḥmad before the year

[1] 1960, i, p. 267.

125 A.H.' But 'there are many instances prior to this date of boys called Muḥammad'. Very rarely is the name Aḥmad met with in the pre-Islamic 'time of ignorance' (*Jāhilīya*), though the name Muḥammad was in common use. Later traditions that the Prophet's name was Aḥmad show that this 'had not always been obvious', though commentators assumed it after about 200.[1]

Dr. Watt then suggests a different interpretation of the *ismu-hu aḥmadu,* namely, that it is to be taken in an adjectival rather than a noun sense. 'For the first century or so of Islam the word *aḥmadu* was regarded not as a proper name but as a simple adjective. The clause in question can then be translated "announcing the good tidings of a messenger who will come after me whose name is worthy of more praise".' The reference may be to John 14,17, 'the Spirit of truth ... abideth with you'. 'Alternatively, if *aḥmadu* is taken to mean more attribution of praise, there might be a reference to the words "he shall glorify me" (Jn. 16,14).' In any case, 'there are strong grounds for holding' that the identification of Aḥmad with the name of Muḥammad 'was not commonly accepted by Muslims until the first half of the second century'. This theory is supported by J. Schacht in the new *Encyclopaedia of Islam* who says, 'it has been concluded that the word aḥmad in Qur'ān 61,6 is to be taken not as a proper name but as an adjective ... and that it was understood as a proper name only after Muḥammad had been identified with the Paraclete'.

Even if *aḥmadu* is to be taken as an adjective, there remains the sentence 'announcing the good tidings of a messenger who will come after me, whose name is worthy of praise'. How can this be interpreted? It is a clear reference to the Gospel, for Jesus is declared to have said this, and the resemblances to the Gospel according to John are close. In the Gospel Jesus promised the Paraclete four times (Jn. 14,16; 14,26; 15,26; 16,7). He said: 'I will pray the Father, and he will give you another Comforter, that he may be with you for ever, even the Spirit of truth ... the Comforter, even the Holy Spirit, whom the Father will send in my name, he shall teach you all things ... the Comforter ... even the Spirit of truth ... shall bear witness

[1] art. 'His Name is Ahmad', in *The Muslim World*, xliii, pp. 110ff.

of me.' The promise is unmistakably that of the Holy Spirit, the Spirit of truth, which was to come to the disciples from the Day of Pentecost onwards, bear witness of Christ, and lead into more truth.

That is the primary meaning. But that the Holy Spirit comes in later messengers cannot be denied. The idea of a succession of prophets is found both in Bible and Qur'ān. Early Christian apology declared that Jesus was the prophet promised by Moses (Acts 7,37). A similar hope is found in fragments from the Dead Sea Scrolls and shows that the expectation was current among the Jews before Christian times.[1] In the context of sūra 61 Moses is spoken of first protesting against infidelity, then Jesus whose Evidences were rejected, then Muḥammad who came with 'guidance and the religion of truth'. In an earlier sura the 'native' or 'illiterate' prophet was said to have been mentioned in the Torah and the Gospel. (7,156/157) Muḥammad sought to bear witness to Jesus, by protecting him from slander, and showing the truth against error and division; the Qur'ān itself was sent to 'confirm the Book which was before it' and to act as 'a protector over it'. (5,52/48) Every true Messenger must be inspired by the Spirit of God, and this divine Spirit remains with the believing community.

(c) Similarities

The above passage has been considered at length since it is in dispute, and is partly a quotation from the Gospel. There are many other verses of the Qur'ān which remind the reader of some Gospel passage or passages. Some of the most striking will now be mentioned briefly.

2,24/26: 'God is not ashamed to coin an occasional parable (from) a gnat or any thing higher;' etc. Mark 4,11f.: 'Unto them which are without all things are done in parables.' Matt. 23,24: 'Strain out the gnat and swallow the camel.'

2,266/264: 'He may be compared to a smooth rock with earth upon it – a heavy rain falls upon it and leaves it bare.' Luke 6.49: 'A house upon the earth without founda-

[1] E. F. F. Bishop, 'The Qumran Scrolls and the Qur'ān', in *The Muslim World*, 1958, pp. 232f.

tion; against which the stream broke and straightway it fell in.'

3,24/25: 'Each will be paid in full what he has earned, without being wronged.' Matt. 20,8ff.: 'Pay them their hire, beginning at the first unto the last.' See also Romans 6,23.

3,25/26: 'O God, owner of the (kingly) power, thou givest the power to whom thou willst, and withdrawest the power from whom thou willst.' Matt. 21,43: 'The kingdom of God shall be taken away from you.' Lk. 18,14: 'Every one that exalteth himself shall be humbled.'

4,141/142: 'When they stand up for the Prayer, they stand up lazily, making a show before the people.' Matt. 6,5: 'They love to stand and pray . . . that they may be seen of men.'

5,82/78: 'Those of the Children of Israel who disbelieved were cursed by the tongue of David and Jesus, son of Mary.' Matt. 23,13ff.: 'Woe unto you, scribes and Pharisees, hypocrites, because ye shut the kingdom of heaven against men.'

7,38/40: 'For those who have counted our signs false and been too proud to receive them, the gates of heaven will not be opened, nor will they enter the garden, until a camel pass through the eye of a needle.' Mark 10,25: 'It is easier for a camel to go through the eye of a needle, than for a rich man to enter the kingdom of God.'

7,42f./44f.: 'Between the two (parties) of them is a partition . . . The inmates of the Fire shall call to the inmates of the Garden: Cause some of the water or of what God hath provided for you to overflow upon us.' Luke 16,24ff.: 'Send Lazarus, that he may dip the tip of his finger in water . . . between us and you there is a great gulf fixed.'

7,178/179: 'Hearts have they but they understand not with them; eyes have they but they see not with them; ears have they but they hear not with them.' Matt. 13,13: 'Seeing they see not, and hearing they hear not, neither do they understand.'

7,186: 'They ask thee about the Hour . . . The knowledge of it is with my Lord only . . . it comes to you not otherwise than suddenly.' Luke 17,20f.: 'Being asked . . . when the kingdom of God cometh, he answered . . . the kingdom of God is within you.' Also Mark 13,32ff.: 'Of that day or of that hour knoweth no one . . . but the Father . . . lest coming suddenly.' Also Acts 1,7.

9,81/80: 'Even if thou ask pardon for them seventy times, God will not pardon them.' Matt. 18,21f.: 'How oft shall I forgive, until seven times? . . . Until seventy times seven.'

9,112/111: 'God hath bought from the believers their persons . . . killing and being killed – a promise binding upon Him in the Torah, the Gospel, and the Qur'ān.' Matt. 5,11f.: 'Blessed are ye when men shall reproach you, and persecute you . . . for great is your reward in heaven.'

16,109/107: 'They have loved the life of this world more than the Hereafter.' 1 John 2,15: 'Love not the world, neither the things that are in the world . . . the world passeth away, and the lust thereof: but he that doeth the will of God abideth for ever.'

17,14/13: 'We shall bring forth to him on the resurrection-day a book.' Rev. 20,12: 'the dead were judged out of the things which were written in the books.'

18,47/49: 'The Book will be placed in position.' As above.

23,103/101: 'When the trumpet shall be blown, there will be no (claims of) lineage amongst them.' Mark 12,25: 'When they shall rise from the dead, they neither marry, nor are given in marriage.'

24,61: 'When ye enter houses, salute each other with a blessed and good wish of life from God.' Matt. 10,12f.: 'As ye enter into a house salute it. And if the house be worthy let your peace come upon it.'

29,60: 'How many a beast bears not its own provision, but God provideth for it and for you.' Matt. 6,26: 'Behold the birds of the heaven, that they sow not, neither do they reap, nor gather into barns; and your heavenly Father feedeth them.'

36,12ff./13f.: 'Coin a parable for them: The people of a town when the envoys came to it; when we sent to them two, and they held them as liars; then we emphasized by a third . . . It was said, "Enter the Garden",' etc. Matt. 21,33ff.: 'Hear another parable: There was a man that was a householder which . . . let it out to husbandmen . . . And the husbandmen took his servants, and beat one, and killed another, and stoned another.'

39,30/29: 'God hath coined a similitude – a man who belongs to (several) partners at variance with each other, and a man wholly belonging to one man, are they to be compared to the same thing?' Matt. 6,24: 'No man can serve two masters: for either he will hate the one and love the other; or else he will hold to one and despise the other.'

46,19/20: 'You made away with your good things in your worldly life and enjoyed them, so today you will be recompensed the punishment of humiliation for having set up to be great in the earth without justification.' Luke 16,25: 'Remember that thou in thy lifetime receivedst thy good things . . . but now . . . thou art in anguish.'

56,8f.: 'Those on the right hand, what are they? Those on the left hand, what are they?' Matt. 25,33: 'He shall set the sheep on his right hand, but the goats on the left.'

57,12f.: 'On the day when one will see the believers male and female with their light running before them and at their right hands . . . On the day when the Hypocrites, male and female, will say to those who have believed, "Wait for us; let us borrow some of your light"; it will be said: "Turn back again and seek light"; between them will be set a wall with a door in it; inside will be mercy, and outside it, in front of it the punishment.' Matt. 25,1ff.: 'Ten virgins, which took their lamps . . . and five of them were foolish, and five were wise . . . And the foolish said unto the wise, "Give us of your oil" . . . But the wise answered . . . "Go to those that sell and buy for yourselves." And while they went away . . . the door was shut.'

58,8/7: 'God knoweth what is in the heavens and what is in the earth. There is not a private conclave of three, but he is a fourth in it.' Matt. 18,20: 'Where two or three are gathered together in my name, there am I in the midst of them.'

There are many other words of the Qur'ān which recall words of the Bible, both Old and New Testaments, in religious and ethical teaching. There are stories and words of Adam, Abraham, Moses and other prophets. There are quotations, such as 21,105: 'And we have written in the Psalms, after the reminder: "Inherit the earth shall my servants the righteous".' Descriptions of the judgement and the future life recall the books of Revelation, Ezekiel and Daniel.

What have been given above are some of the most obvious Quranic parallels to words in the Gospels. Later writers, Bukhārī, Ṭabarī, and many others, gained a considerable knowledge of the Gospels and of Christian story, though they tended to recount the marvellous and often the apocryphal. This is not in the Qur'ān, which refers back to the teaching of Jesus in the Gospel and seeks to preserve it. It is the Gospel teaching that needs study, for both Jesus and Muḥammad deplored those who sought after vulgar signs and neglected their teaching, those who 'call me Lord, Lord, and do not the things which I say'. (Luke 6,46)

11

The Death of Jesus

WHAT does the Qur'ān mean in its words about the death of Jesus? This question has been debated down the ages by Muslims and Christians.

> The first reference is the Meccan sūra 19,34/33: 'Peace is upon me the day of my birth, and the day of my death, and the day of my being raised up alive.'

This verse speaks of the death of Jesus, which would seem to agree naturally with other verses on the true humanity of the Son of Mary. Being 'raised up alive' might refer to the Gospel story of the resurrection of Jesus. However, the interpretation must be taken along with the earlier verse 19,15, addressed to Zachariah about John the Baptist in virtually the same terms: 'Peace is upon him the day of his birth, and the day of his death, and the day of his being raised up alive.' Here the resurrection would be the general resurrection at the end of the world.

Because of the difficulty of reconciling this verse about Jesus with a later one (4,156/157) early Islam soon interpreted his death as to occur after his second coming. Baiḍāwī said that after the future descent of Jesus he would remain for forty years and then die and be buried by Muslims. This burial, legend has long held, would be at Medina (see later, page 124). It must be said that the Qur'ān knows nothing of these elaborations. There is no futurity in the grammar of the Qur'ān (19,34/33) to suggest a post-millennial death. The plain meaning seems to be his physical death at the end of his present human life on earth.

Next, in the Medinan verse 3,48/55 we read: '(Recall) when God said: "O Jesus, I am going to bring thy term to an end and raise thee to myself, and purify thee from those who have disbelieved; and I am going to set those who have followed thee above those who have disbelieved until the day of resurrection; then to me do ye return and I shall judge between you in regard to that in which ye have been differing".'

'Bring thy term to an end' or 'take thee to me' (*mutawaffīka*) is taken to mean 'cause thee to die'. It is used of men dying (2,241/240), and of believers being called to God in the night, raised up to complete a stated term and returning to him. (6,60)

This same verb is used again of Jesus in 5,117: 'I was a witness over them as long as I remained amongst them, but when thou didst take me to thyself, it was thou who wert a watcher over them.' So that in two verses the return of Jesus to God is spoken of, and his death clearly in 19,34/33.

The commentators have had trouble over these verses since they have let themselves be dominated by 4,156/157 which they assumed denied the crucifixion. So Baiḍāwī gave five alternative meanings for 3,48/55: it could mean 'achieve the whole of thy term and tarry till thy appointed end', or 'take thee from the earth', or 'take thee to myself sleeping', or 'destroy in thee the lusts which hinder ascent to the world of spirits', or 'some say that God let him die for seven hours and then raised him to heaven'. This last was said to be held by Christians, but perhaps Baiḍāwī felt that the passage compelled some kind of belief in an actual death.

In an important study of this question a modern writer says that in 3,48/55 'God is addressing Jesus and says, "Truly I am he who calls you to death" or "It is I who am causing you to die". The construction is the active participle with the pronoun (object) attached. It is followed by the active participle of the verb *rafa*ʿ (raise) . . . The same verb is used in sura 4,157 . . . The deepest point arising from 3,48/55 is the question whether "I am causing you to die and I will receive you beyond death unto myself", may not well describe the actual experience of Jesus in the climax of the rejection that came to its fulness in the

Cross. If so, then the passage relates, not to a still future and post-millenial death (which puts it right outside the immediate context of the Injīl's events to which the present force of 3,48/55 seems to relate) but rather . . . in terms belonging to its inwardness as experienced by Jesus.'[1] In other words, the cross was both anticipated by Jesus and was an actual event in which he really died. The verse continues, 'I will . . . purify thee [or 'clear thee'] from those who have disbelieved'. This vindication of Jesus would be that after his death God raised him to himself.

A fourth reference to the death of Jesus may be seen in 5,19/17: 'Assuredly they have disbelieved who say that God is

> the Messiah, son of Mary; say: "Who then will control God in the least if he wisheth to destroy the Messiah, son of Mary, and his mother, and those who are on the earth altogether, seeing that to God belongs the sovereignty of the heavens and the earth?" '

If this word was spoken, as some think, in reply to the Christians of Najrān, or to correct their differing views, then it is understandable as asserting the true humanity and the death of Jesus. Ibn Isḥāq spoke of 'using their own arguments against them in reference to their master to show them their error thereby. "God there is no God but he", no associate with him in his authority. "The Living the Ever-existent", the living who cannot die, whereas Jesus died and was crucified according to their doctrine.'[2] So by the Christian belief in the real death of Jesus his true humanity is affirmed. God cannot die, and God is not the Messiah, for he could destroy the Messiah if he willed.

There is a possible further reference in 5,79/75: 'The Messiah, son of Mary, is nothing but a messenger before whose time the messengers have passed away.' Bell expands this in a note to imply, 'as he also passed away like them'. On the other hand 5,110 says, 'when I restrained the Children of Israel from thee'. But a modern commentator, Yusuf 'Alī, remarks that 'the Jews were seeking to take the life of Jesus long before their final attempt to crucify him'. Several times in the Gospel they tried

[1] 'Abd al-Tafāhum, 'The Qur'ān and the Holy Communion', in *The Muslim World*, 1959, pp. 242ff.
[2] *Life of Muhammad*, p. 272.

to stone Jesus before the final organized onslaught of the crucifixion.

The critical passage which, on the face of it, seems to contradict the other Quranic verses which speak of the death of Jesus is 4,154–157/155–159. This is so important that it must be given in full. 'So for their [Jews'] violating their compact, and for their unbelief in the signs of God, their killing the prophets without justification, and for their unbelief, and their speaking against Mary a mighty slander; and for their saying: "We killed the Messiah, Jesus, son of Mary, the messenger of God", though they did not kill him and did not crucify him, but he was counterfeited for them; verily those who have gone different ways in regard to him are in doubt about him; they have no (revealed) knowledge of him and only follow opinion; though they did not certainly kill him. Nay, God raised him to himself. God is sublime, wise. And there is no People of the Book but will surely believe in him before his death, and on the day of resurrection, he will be regarding them a witness.'

It is important to study the context of this passage, which is that of the rejection of the messengers of God by the Jews, the first People of the Book. They had broken the covenant sent by Moses, killed the prophets, slandered Mary, and claimed to have killed the Messiah by themselves. This is strongly denied. God himself could kill the Messiah (see 5,19/17), but men could not do so against his will for, as it is often said, God is 'the best of plotters' who overthrows human plots. The final sentence (4,157/159) may mean that no one of the People of the Book, Jews and Christians, but will believe in Jesus before his (or their) death. The ambiguity of 'his' led some commentators to say that Jesus is still living in the body and will appear to convince men before his final death. But the intention of the verse is clear, to show that all must believe in Jesus, and he will witness concerning them at the resurrection.

Similarly, 4,156/157 is to defend the Messiah against those Jews who maintained that they (alone) had killed and crucified him, and therefore that he could not be the Messiah. 'They did not crucify him' (*mā ṣalabū-hu*) may be translated 'they did not cause his death on the cross'. And Bell's rather harsh translation 'he was counterfeited for them' (*shubbiha la-hum*), has also been translated as 'it appeared to them as such' (Massignon), or 'only a likeness of that was shown to them' (Arberry). Ubayy b. Ka'b read in his version of the Qur'ān, 'and they who entertained wrong opinions about him, did not crucify him'.

Traditional Muslim interpretation has been that the Jews tried to kill Jesus but were unable to do so. One story tells of Jesus hiding in a niche in a wall and one of his companions being killed in his place. This may refer to the two places in the Gospel, before the crucifixion, where Jesus avoided enemies to escape premature death. (Luke 4,30; John 8,59) Another popular story, recounted by Wahb, tells of the betrayal of Jesus by Judas, the trial, and the preparation of the cross. But then it is said that the cloud of darkness came down, God sent angels to protect Jesus, and Judas was crucified in his place. Then God caused Jesus to die for three hours, after which he was raised to heaven. This gives part of the Gospel story, though angelic aid was rejected and Jesus was crucified for three hours before the darkness descended, and after three more hours he expired.[1]

Two distinct questions emerge: Did Jesus really die on the cross? Was there a substitute who suffered in his place? There is no doubt that the canonical Gospels all affirm the first and have no suggestion of the second. The four Gospels agree in the real death of Jesus on the cross, and give the centurion's witness to this. (Mk. 15,45) John adds the piercing of his side with a spear. But there early arose in some Christian circles a reluctance to believe that Jesus, as a divine being and Son of God, could really die. Ignatius, writing about A.D. 115, said that some believed that Jesus 'suffered in semblance'. The apocryphal Gospel of Peter in the second century said that on the cross Jesus 'was silent, since he felt no pain', and at the end 'the Lord cried out, saying, "My power, my power, you have left me". And when he spoke he was taken up.' This is a perversion of the Gospel which said that he 'gave up the ghost' or expired. The apocryphal Acts of John, about the middle of the second century, said that Jesus appeared to John in a cave during the crucifixion and said, 'John, unto the multitude below in Jerusalem I am

[1] A. Jeffery, *A Reader on Islam*, pp. 592f.; *Christ in Islam*, pp. 40f.

being crucified and pierced with lances and reeds, and gall and vinegar is given me to drink. But unto thee I speak.' And later it is said, 'Nothing, therefore of the things which they will say of me have I suffered . . . I was pierced, yet I was not smitten; hanged, and I was not hanged; that blood flowed from me, and it flowed not'.[1]

These and later writers were Docetic, they held that Jesus in his person, or at least in his suffering, only 'seemed' (*dokein*) to be physical. Needless to say, this is not the point of view of the Qur'ān or the Gospel. Yet there are two verses in the epistles which might already have suggested ambiguity about the humanity of Jesus. Phil. 2,7: 'made in the likeness of men'; Heb. 2,17: 'made like his brethren.' 'Likeness' is not the same as identity.

Some Muslim commentators found support for the idea of a substitute who was crucified in the teachings of the famous Egyptian Gnostic Christian Basilides, who lived in the second century. Basilides is said to have written a Gospel, though it was more likely a commentary. Unfortunately his ideas are only known through the writings of his opponents, and these differ considerably. The orthodox Irenaeus, about 185, said that Basilides taught that the divine Nous (intelligence) appeared in human form, but at the crucifixion he changed forms with Simon of Cyrene who had carried the cross; the Jews took Simon and nailed him to the cross instead of Jesus who stood by deriding them for their error before ascending to heaven. Clement of Alexandria, however, about 215, said that Basilides taught that the humanity of Jesus could be tainted with sin, and he rejected the notion of the crucifixion of Simon. And Hippolytus (d. 235) said that Basilides had taught that it was an essential condition of redemption that Christ should pass through all grades of existence, and this included death.[2]

Though rejected by the orthodox Christians the idea of a substitute survived on the borderline. The influential Persian teacher Mani (d. 276) called Jesus 'son of the widow', and seems

[1] J. B. Lightfoot, *The Apostolic Fathers*, pp. 156f.; *Apocryphal New Testament*, pp. 91, 254f.; R. M. Grant and D. N. Freedman, *The Secret Sayings of Jesus*, p. 38.

[2] J. Doresse, *Secret Books of the Egyptian Gnostics*, pp. 22f.

to have thought that the widow's son of Nain, whom Jesus had raised, was finally put to death in his place. Another Manichaean document taught that the Devil, who was hoping to have Jesus crucified, himself fell a victim to the crucifixion. A late Gospel of Barnabas was also supposed to have influenced thinking on this point, but it has been clearly shown that it was unknown, even to Muslim apologetics, till the sixteenth century.[1]

The idea of a substitute for the crucifixion has been adopted by many Muslim writers. Not only Simon of Cyrene, but Judas, Pilate, a disciple, or even an enemy of Jesus have been suggested for this office. Baiḍāwī said that when the Jews gathered to kill Jesus, God thereupon informed him that he would take him up to heaven. Jesus then asked his disciples which of them would be willing to have his likeness cast upon him and be killed and enter paradise. One of them accepted and God put the likeness of Jesus upon him and he was crucified. It is said also that he was the one who betrayed Jesus. That Judas committed suicide about the time of the crucifixion may have been one source of this belief. Ṭabarī said that Herod gave the order to kill Jesus but he hid himself. Simon then denied him and another betrayed him; Jesus was seized and dragged away to a cross. The Jews had a chief called Joshua and God took Jesus out of their sight, and gave his form and appearance to Joshua who was crucified in his place despite his protests. Joshua stayed on the cross for seven days, and each night Mary, the mother of Jesus, came and wept at the foot of the cross, but on the eighth day Jesus descended from heaven to Mary and his disciples. Christians celebrate this descent and return to heaven as a feast. The king of Rome, who became a Christian after destroying Jerusalem, took the wood on which it was said Jesus had been crucified and made a chapel (*qibla*) of it. But it was not Jesus who had been nailed to that tree but one who resembled him, and God had raised Jesus to heaven. Qur'ān and Christian story are quoted in support of this romancing, but it is evident that there is little scriptural about it.

Although the idea of a substitute has slender foundations yet

[1] T. Andrae, *Mohammed*, 1936, p. 157. J. Jomier, 'L'Evangile selon Barnabé', in *Mélanges de l'Institut Dominicain d'Etudes Orientales*, 1959, pp. 137ff.

it has been taught down the ages and is repeated today. For example, the Egyptian writer ʻAbd al-Ḥamīd Judah al-Saḥḥār in his novel *The Messiah, Jesus Son of Mary*, published in 1952, thought that Jesus was not crucified but Judas suffered in his place. Yet his book, printed in Cairo by Muslims, shows on the cover Jesus wearing the crown of thorns.

However, there are signs of different opinions. One of the most outstanding modern writers, Dr. Kamel Hussein, says, 'the idea of a substitute for Christ is a very crude way of explaining the Quranic text. They had to explain a lot to the masses. No cultured Muslim believes in this nowadays. The text is taken to mean that the Jews thought they killed Christ but God raised him unto him in a way we can leave unexplained among the several mysteries which we have taken for granted on faith alone.'[1]

In fact, it must be made quite plain that the Qur'ān itself does not say that Jesus suffered in a false body (in the Docetic fashion), nor does it say that a substitute was made so that somebody else suffered in his place. Any later addition to this is unjustifiable and a perversion of the text. All that 4,156/157 says is *shubbiha la-hum*, either 'he was counterfeited for them', or, better, 'it appeared to them as such'.

Commenting on this verse ʻAbd al-Tafāhum says that on any and every interpretation of the 'apparentness' of Christ's sufferings (Docetic, Gnostic, Aḥmadiyyah, popular or hypothetical), it is incontrovertible that Jesus was a teacher whom men intended should suffer. Substitution has no relevance where there is no victim in the situation. *Shubbiha* 'at least is the plainest possible witness to crucifixion as the sought-for fate of Jesus . . . Perhaps then after all there is something that might need a memorial feast?' The institution of the Last Supper, according to this writer, is justified on Quranic as well as Biblical grounds; it is the ʻ*īd*, the festival of sūra 5,114. 'The prospective side of the cross . . . is to this extent the same whether we follow the Biblical or the Quranic Jesus . . . For are we to suppose that Jesus went artificially into this encounter well aware of the impending 'rescue', or whatever *shubbiha* is finally taken to mean? Would

[1] *City of Wrong*, p. 222.

not that reduce the whole situation to bathos?'[1] It can be strongly argued that while the Jews thought they alone had crucified Jesus in fact the power was not in their hands, only God could kill the Messiah.

If there was no substitute then did Jesus really die? This is the hardest problem, on Quranic grounds, in this whole complex question. Some modern Muslim writers think that Jesus was crucified but did not die on the cross. Thus Sayyid Aḥmad Khān said, 'crucifixion itself does not cause the death of a man, because only the palms of his hands, or the palms of his hands and feet are pierced . . . After three or four hours Christ was taken down from the cross, and it is certain that at that moment he was still alive. Then the disciples concealed him in a very secret place, out of fear of the enmity of the Jews.' M. 'Alī also says that Jesus was only on the cross for a few hours, the two thieves were not dead either when taken down, and Jesus also was taken away by his friends, and later appeared in disguise or in hiding. This leads on to his Aḥmadiyya belief that Jesus wandered away before going to Kashmir where he finally died.[2] According to the Gospel, however, Jesus was on the cross for over six hours, and was certainly dead when taken down. (Mk. 15,37–45)

Others take a different line and say that Jesus died indeed, but his death was only of the body, like that of all true servants of God and martyrs of Islam. Sūra 2,149/154 says: 'Say not of those who may be killed in the way of God, "Dead"; nay, (they are) alive, only ye are not aware.' And 3,163/169 says: 'Count not those who have been killed in the way of God as dead, nay, alive with their Lord, provided for.' Others also say that what the Jews could not kill was the soul of Jesus. As it says in the Gospel, 'be not afraid of those who kill the body, but are not able to kill the soul; but rather fear him who is able to destroy both soul and body'. (Matt. 10,28)

A profound and imaginative interpretation of the crucifixion from a modern Muslim point of view is that by Dr. Kamel

[1] 'The Qur'ān and the Holy Communion', *Muslim World*, 1959, pp. 242f.

[2] *Religious Ideas of Sir Sayyid Aḥmad Khān*; M. 'Alī, *Holy Qur'ān*, p. 231. For a critical study of this idea see H. J. Fisher, *Ahmadiyya*, 1963, pp. 68ff.

Hussein in *City of Wrong*. The English translator, Kenneth Cragg, says that the theme of the crucifixion 'has here been sensitively explored and presented, probably for the first time by a thinker within the faith of Islam'. City of Wrong, Qaryah Zālimah, is a Quranic phrase occurring in 21,11; 22,44/45, and 22,47/48. 21,11 reads: 'How many a town which was doing wrong have we broken up, and set up after it another people?' This recalls Matthew 21,43: 'The kingdom of God shall be taken away from you and given to a nation bringing forth the fruits thereof.' In this book the City of Wrong is Jerusalem, though it stands for all mankind; and the whole book is concerned with one day, the fatal day of Good Friday. After a most careful and sympathetic study, in the manner of a historical novel or dialogue, which shows close knowledge of the Gospel in that Caiaphas, Pilate, the disciples, and other characters appear, the conclusion of this book is that Jesus was condemned, led out to be crucified, darkness covered the land for three hours, and when the cloud lifted the Christ was no longer there. 'There is one thing about the events of this day of which I am aware which you do not know. It is that God has raised the Lord Christ to himself. He was the light of God upon the earth. The people of Jerusalem would have nothing to do with him except to extinguish the light. Whereupon God has darkened the world around them.'[1]

It has been noted that Dr Hussein rejects the notion of a substitute for Jesus. But he goes further, beyond the debates on the events to the meaning and intention. 'It [or 'he'] appeared to them as such' (4,156/157) could refer either to the crucifixion ('it') or to Jesus ('he'), either that Jesus did not die on the cross, or never came to the cross at all. The significance of the cross Dr Hussein sees to be in that men did crucify Jesus in intention, all their actions were bent towards it, and they utterly rejected the Christ of God. Dr Cragg comments that if we 'concentrate on the event as something which was intended for Jesus, the whole of the human significance of the decision against him and for his death, as taken by his contemporaries, remains unimpaired. . . . The author remains strictly within his

[1] *City of Wrong*, E. T. Amsterdam 1959, London 1960, pp. lx, 183.

Quranic grounds. The interesting thing is that few, if any, before him have taken a specifically Muslim initiative to study the Christian history on its manward side. One clear result of his work is to remind Christians that they should think again before they crudely and hastily assert that the Muslim holy book denies the Cross. In a very crucial sense it affirms it. For the Cross is not only a redemptive deed, it is also, seen from the manward side, the deed of rejection in which men registered their verdict against the life and personality of Jesus.'[1]

In a sixty-four page review of *City of Wrong* Fr. G. C. Anawati makes as one of his few but important criticisms that it 'reduces Christianity to a teaching taken from the Gospel, transmitted by Jesus'. He prefers the 'hidden teachings' of Jesus found in John's Gospel, though this is the least reliable of the four Gospels for the actual words of Jesus, according to many critical scholars. But Anawati insists that 'for Christians the death of Christ is an absolutely essential truth, the foundation of their doctrine'.[2]

The Qur'ān asserts both the rejection of Christ by man, and the power of God. Human sin in trying to destroy the Messiah is met by divine power, so that men could not hold to their victim. As Peter said on the day of Pentecost, 'it was not possible' that Jesus 'should be held' by death. (Acts 2,24) And it is said several times in the Qur'ān that men 'kill the prophets wrongfully'. (3,20/21; 2,85/91; 4,154/155)

Mention has been made of other Quranic verses which speak of the death of Jesus. 5,117: 'Take me to thyself' or 'cause me to die' (*tawaffaitani*) has often been interpreted of Jesus dying at some future time, after his second coming. But on this Dr Maḥmūd Shaltūt, late Rector of Al Azhar university, said, 'the expression *tawaffaitani* is entitled in this verse to bear the meaning of ordinary death . . . There is no way to interpret "death" as occurring after his return from heaven in the supposition that he is now alive in heaven, because the verse very clearly limits the connexion of Jesus to his connexion with his own people of his own day and the connexion is not with the people living at the time when he returns . . . All that the verses referring to this

[1] *City of Wrong*, p. xii.
[2] *Mélanges de l'Institut Dominicain d'Etudes Orientales*, 1955.

subject mean is that God promised Jesus that he would complete for him his life-span and would raise him up to himself.'[1]

Although Islam traditionally denied the crucifixion as a fact, whereas orthodox Christianity affirmed it strongly, yet it is curious that Islam insisted firmly on the true humanity of Jesus, while the later church often almost forgot this in stressing the divinity of Christ. Only in modern times has the full significance of the humanity of Jesus been recognized again, and now Christians realize this more keenly perhaps than any generation since the first century.

K. Cragg emphasizes that 'the Qur'ān does not dispute that the Jews desired to crucify Jesus. The fact that they resisted him strongly and resented his words is another instance in the Muslim mind of that hostility on the part of gainsayers to which all the prophets from Noah to Muḥammad were exposed.' Nor does the Qur'ān name a substitute who died in the place of Jesus. Indeed, 'what are we to say of the nature of a God who behaves in this way or of the character of a Christ who permits another – even if a Judas – to suffer the consequences of an antagonism his own teaching has raised against himself? . . . Christian history believes that Jesus suffered the full length of that hostility, and that he did so willingly, as the price of loyalty to his own message . . . Not rendering evil for evil, nor countering hatred with guile.'[2]

Force is added to the modern stress on the historicity of the life and death of Jesus, by the fact that secular historians also accept the crucifixion as a fact. No serious modern historian doubts that Jesus was a historical figure and that he was crucified, whatever he may think of the faith in the resurrection.

Because of this some Muslim writers have tried to take the question of the death of Jesus beyond the fact to its interpretation. Years ago H. A. R. Gibb said that Islam 'is distinguished from Christianity, not so much (in spite of all outward appearances) by its repudiation of the trinitarian concept of the Unity of God, as by its rejection of the soteriology of Christian doctrine and the relics of the old nature cults which survived in the rites

[1] Quoted in *The Muslim World*, xxxiv, pp. 214f.

[2] *The Call of the Minaret*, 1956, pp. 294ff.

and practices of the Christian Church'. And Dr Hussein puts a similar idea in a different way: 'I contend that the Apostles on that day had no idea of the Divine significance of Crucifixion or that it had been decreed from eternity. They had no idea of redemption, Atonement or the role of Jesus Christ as Saviour. All this (I hope I am not wrong here) was defined and explained clearly by that most remarkable of men, St Paul.'[1]

Some have gone further, as if the happening of the crucifixion was a minor matter. Fatḥī 'Uthmān said, 'the matter of the crucifixion is not simply the occurrence of a certain historical event in one form or another. It is a matter of the consequence deduced from that event, by which we mean the idea of salvation.'[2] Others have said that the debate about the actuality of the crucifixion is 'quite unfortunate and fruitless'. Yet either it happened or it did not. And the fact has a vital bearing on the understanding of the life of Jesus, and on the reliability of the Gospel and all the New Testament.

This is not the place to discuss the various teachings of salvation, atonement, sacrifice, substitution, satisfaction, or moral example, that have been associated with the crucifixion at different periods of church history. That would require another volume and far fuller treatment. St Paul did not 'define' all this, and no one theory has been adopted by the churches or written into the creeds. But in the Bible pardon and salvation are seen throughout as the free gift of God bestowed upon human repentance. Isaiah repented and was cleansed from his sin. (Isa. 6,7) So was the Psalmist. (Ps. 7f.) Ezekiel declared that if the wicked turned from his evil ways and did that which was right he would live, for God has no pleasure in the death of the wicked, but seeks his return. (Ezek. 18,21–23) This prophetic message is continued in the New Testament. Jesus brought health to body and soul by declaring the forgiveness of God. (Mk. 2,5; Lk. 7,47, etc.) Far from needing reconciliation God, said Paul, 'was in Christ reconciling the world unto himself'. (2 Cor. 5.19) God is always the prime mover; 'while we were yet sinners Christ died for us'. (Rom. 5,8) There is emphasis upon

[1] *Mohammedanism*, 1949, p. 69; *City of Wrong*, p. 224.
[2] See review in *The Muslim World*, liii, p. 253.

the universality of God, his unchanging goodness and his unbounded grace towards all men in all ages. There is some kinship between Quranic and Biblical belief here; see sura 93,6–8: 'Did he not find thee an orphan and give thee shelter? Did he not find thee erring, and guide thee? Did he not find thee poor, and enrich thee?' In the medieval church legalistic views of atonement served to obscure the simple Biblical view of the nature of God, his love for men, his forgiveness of the penitent, and his revelation in love in Jesus. But the Biblical teachings are still there and must determine our view of the forgiveness and salvation that God offers.

In conclusion, attention must be turned again to the interpretation of sūra 4,156/157. It has sometimes been said that this verse, or Islamic interpretation of it, was influenced by Docetic teaching. But it is not clear how far Docetic and Gnostic teachings were known or were alive in Arabia of the seventh century. Some of the earlier Muslim historians were reluctant to make assertions about what happened at the cross, in contrast to the later writers who spoke freely of a substitute being crucified. Basilides and the Docetic Gospels had flourished in the second Christian century. In the fifth century there were the 'aphthartodocetists', to whom the emperor Justinian belonged and he tried to enforce their views that Christ was so glorified that his body was insensible to fleshly weakness and incorruptible. Even Justinian, however, did not deny the crucifixion, for he was one of those responsible for the formula 'God was crucified for us'. This was pointed out by the Caliph Mahdī, about A.D. 781, in his controversy with the Nestorian Patriarch Timothy, and Timothy protested that like other Nestorians he rejected this heresy. 'It is clear that it is the human nature of the Word-God which suffered and died, because in no book of the prophets or the Gospel do we find that God himself died in the flesh, though we do find that the Son and Jesus Christ died in the flesh. The expression that "God suffered in the flesh" is not correct.'[1]

The sharp distinction between the human Jesus and the Christ has no place in the Qur'ān, nor in the Bible, and the

[1] J. W. Sweetman, *Islam and Christian Theology*, i, pp. 31, 79; from A. Mingana, *Timothy's Apology for Christianity*.

Qur'ān denies Adoptionist theories that God had taken to himself offspring. It does not say that somebody else suffered in the place of Jesus, or that Jesus could not die. Can it then have been influenced by Docetic ideas in saying that 'they did not kill and did not crucify him'? This has often been the view of Christian commentators. But Y. Moubarac has said that beyond textual resemblances one must 'verify the relationship of intentions and doctrines'. The apparent denial of the real death of Jesus corresponds at first sight to the teachings of Docetism, but one cannot 'conclude with a real relationship, seeing that the Qur'ān is opposed to the discarnate principles of Docetism. Even if the Quranic negation came from Docetic texts it would express a different thing, and this must be emphasized.' M. Rodinson has criticized the method and the over-sympathy of Moubarac, and says that if the idea of the apparent death of Jesus is of Docetic origin, even if it is integrated into a quite different context, that is no doubt interesting and perhaps more important than mere borrowing. But that does not at all destroy the existence of the borrowing; 'respect for the faith of sincere believers must not block or thwart the search for historical truth'.[1]

But is it true? Docetic influence on the Qur'ān is not proved. And it is possible to interpret this passage in a quite different sense.

How then can the passage, 4,156/157, be interpreted? In a penetrating article on this subject some years ago, E. E. Elder remarked that 'the verse does not say that Jesus was not killed, nor was he crucified. It merely states that they (the Jews) did not kill or crucify him. This is true historically, although the responsibility was theirs, the Roman soldiers actually did the work ... But there is another sense in which neither the Romans nor the Jews crucified Jesus. At Pilate's judgement, Jesus answered ... "Thou wouldst have no power against me, except it were given thee from above".' (John 19,11)

On the words *shubbiha la-hum*, this writer comments that 'there is no mention of a substitute here, or anywhere else in the Koran. It seems obvious that it cannot refer to Jesus. It certainly

[1] Y. Moubarac, *Abraham dans le Coran*, 1958, p. 168; M. Rodinson, *Bilan d'études mohammadiennes*, 1963, p. 215.

must refer to something else that has been mentioned. Now the phrase could be translated, "it was made a resemblance to them", or more freely, "it was made a misunderstanding—a perplexity to them". In that case the subject understood would refer to his crucifixion. The verse could then be properly translated, "Yet they slew him not, and they crucified him not – but it (his crucifixion) was made a misunderstanding to them". His crucifixion perplexed them. They saw the event, but failed to appreciate its inner meaning. They even thought they had power over his life'. This would be the meaning of the words which follow in this verse: 'and those who differed about him were in doubt concerning him: no sure knowledge had they about him [or it], but followed only an opinion.'[1]

In the following number of the review in which this article appeared the above interpretation was attacked by an Aḥmadiyya writer, who declared that while Jesus was nailed to the cross he did not die on it; a theory for which there is no evidence in the Qur'ān or Gospel. He declared that 'a Moslem believes Jesus to be the righteous servant of God, and if he were to accept this story of the crucifixion it means that he would have to delete the name of Jesus from the list of the prophets'. But that righteous prophets could be and were killed is mentioned several times in the Qur'ān and at the beginning of this passage, 'their killing the prophets without justification'.[2]

The Jews thought they killed Christ, though 'they did not certainly kill him'. In fact, men could not kill the Messiah, only God could do that, in his mysterious purposes. There is a parallel to this interpretation in sūra 8,17 when the Muslims were rejoicing over the victory at Badr and taking all the credit to themselves. They were sternly reminded that man can do nothing of himself, a doctrine that became deeply rooted in Islam. 'Ye did not kill them but God killed them, and when thou didst throw, it was not thou but God who threw.'[3]

Other verses of the Qur'ān support this interpretation. God indeed can 'destroy the Messiah' (5,19/17). God said: 'O

[1] *The Moslem World*, xiii, pp. 242ff.

[2] M. Din, in *The Moslem World*, xiv, pp. 23ff.

[3] See R. C. Zaehner, *At Sundry Times*, p. 212f.

Jesus, I am going to bring thy term to an end.' (3,48/55) Jesus said: 'when thou didst take me to thyself' (5,117), and 'peace is upon me . . . the day of my death'. (19,34/33) It appeared to the Jews that they alone had killed Jesus, though they were 'in doubt about him'. (4,156/157) To these verses may be added the reference to the Last Supper, 5,114: 'to be to us a festival, to the first and to the last of us, and a sign from thee.' It might be suggested that the Muslim teaching of 'abrogation' (*nāsikh*) could apply to 4,156/157, in view of the numerous contrary verses. 'Abrogation' of one verse of the Qur'ān by another has been accepted in Islam (see suras 2,100/106; 13,39) though generally applied to commands rather than to narratives.

The cumulative effect of the Quranic verses is strongly in favour of a real death, and a complete self-surrender of Jesus. 'From within the experience of Jesus, on every Quranic hypothesis, there was this drawing nigh unto death, this obedience of steadfastness going forward, in loyalty to vocation, into the storm-centre of Jerusalem's bigoted hostility . . . The Quranic Jesus is one whose words and person were rejected, with all the vehemence of Jewry's will to slay . . . Perhaps we have too long allowed the study of all this to be monopolized by anxious controversy over the sequel (which Heaven knows is urgent enough), yet obscuring all the while the immense Quranic implications antecedent to the Cross.'[1]

So in the Gospel the enemies of Jesus mocked him, 'he saved others, himself he cannot save . . . He trusted in God, let him deliver him'. (Matt. 27,43) The submission of Jesus to the will of God, 'even unto the death of the cross', is a major clue to the mystery of his suffering. The deep Semitic religious attitude of utter self-surrender to the will of God is here. Jesus is the *'abd*, the servant, fully surrendered to God and so truly worshipping him. He is the servant of the servants of God, who 'came not to be ministered unto but to minister, and to give his life a ransom for many'. He is the Suffering Servant, 'despised and rejected of men'. He is the Son of Man, the Messiah, truly human, yet exalted, for 'God raised him to himself'.

[1] 'Abd al-Tafāhum, *The Muslim World*, 1959, p. 245.

12

Jesus and the Future

3,48/55: 'God said: "O Jesus, I am going to bring thy term to an end and raise thee to myself [or 'I will take thee to me and I will raise thee to me'], and purify thee from those who have disbelieved; and I am going to set those who have followed thee above those who have disbelieved until the day of resurrection".'

4,156/157: 'God raised him to himself.'

19,34/33: 'The day of my being raised up alive.'

43,61: 'Verily it [or 'he'] is knowledge for the hour.'

The precise meaning of these phrases has found various comment. It has been mentioned that Baiḍāwī on 3,48/55 gave various interpretations: achieve the whole of thy term, or take thee from the earth, or raise thee to heaven. Traditional Islam has thought that Jesus was rapt to heaven, in a fleshly body, though the Qur'ān does not say so. Some thought that Jesus was sent back to earth seven days after his ascension, to send out the disciples, as in the Bible, and then God took him up again to heaven where he will remain till the last day.

The phrase 'God raised him to himself' suggests the Biblical story of the Ascension. But if Jesus is held to have returned to send out the disciples, then the parallel is rather with the resurrection appearances of the Gospel. These are not mentioned in the Qur'ān, but they are not denied, and they agree with the common interpretation. There is a Biblical passage which recalls the Quranic statement, showing that men could not defeat God's plans and so Jesus was exalted. 'He was not abandoned to Hades, and his flesh never suffered corruption . . . The Jesus we speak of has been raised by God, as we can all witness. Exalted thus with God's right hand, he received the Holy Spirit.' (Acts 2,31f.)

A fleshly resurrection of Jesus and bodily ascent to heaven has been held in Christianity. The 'resurrection of the flesh' of all men has been held by Muslims and Christians down to modern times. Today Protestant Christians, at least, prefer to think of the resurrection of the spirit or 'spiritual body' only (as taught by Paul in 1 Cor. 15,44), hence the widespread practice of cremation. In the past Muslims saw no objection to a physical ascension of Jesus to heaven. In the famous story of the night journey of Muḥammad to Jerusalem and ascent to heaven, the Prophet saw in the second heaven Jesus, son of Mary, and John, son of Zachariah. Ibn Isḥāq said that this was a true revelation, 'whether he was asleep or awake'.[1] But some modern Muslim writers say that the ascension of Jesus pertains to his 'social status and not to his geographic position'. Another points out that a bodily ascension must presume a local limitation of God, which runs counter to the concept of his ubiquity. While another says that God took Jesus to himself 'as he takes the souls of the righteous to himself'.[2]

Muslim tradition has long thought that Jesus will come again to restore all things and reign as a just king, and it seems that it was affected by early Christian hopes of a Second Advent. The Qur'ān has none of this, though there are hints which suggest Jesus as an eschatological figure.

3,40/45: 'An eminent one in this word and the hereafter, one of those brought near.'

On this Baiḍāwī commented that the 'eminence' in this world is the prophetic office, in the next the right of intercession. 'According to some what is intended is the high place he is to have in paradise; or his being raised to heaven, and the society of angels.'

4,157/159: 'There is no People of the Book but will surely believe in him before his death, and on the day of resurrection, he will be regarding them a witness.'

[1] *The Life of Muhammad*, pp. 183ff. [2] *Modern Muslim Koran Interpretation*, pp. 70f.

This has been taken to refer to the Jews who would finally accept Jesus despite their having tried to crucify him. Others say that the Jews would only believe in Jesus at the point of their death, too late. Yet others have seen this to mean belief in Christ at his second coming, and so confirmation of his Messiahship. But the verse can apply to all People of the Book, and the resurrection can be after death and not again here on earth.

The most debated verse is 43,61: 'The Son of Mary is used as a parable . . . Verily it [or 'he'] is knowledge for the hour.' A canonical variation allows the reading of *'alam*, 'mark' or 'signal', for *'ilm*, 'knowledge'. In this reading the second coming of Jesus would be a 'signal' of the last hour. But it is just as easy, and perhaps more legitimate, to translate 'it' of the Qur'ān or message which gave knowledge of the Hour in the time of Muḥammad. Nevertheless, on the slender basis of the variant some traditions and commentaries elaborated theories of the coming of Jesus. Bukhārī in his version of the Traditions said that the Son of Mary would descend among men as a just judge. He would break the crosses, kill the swine, suppress the poll-tax, and make wealth so abundant that nobody would wish for any more. Baiḍāwī said that Jesus would descend in the Holy Land, that he would kill al-Dajjāl, the Anti-Christ, and go to Jerusalem, worshipping there, killing swine and all who do not believe in him, reign in peace for forty years, and finally die and be buried in Medina. An empty place beside the tomb of Muḥammad in Medina was thought to be reserved for Jesus.

These are later fabrications, though they have been popularly held down the ages. Nowadays opinions vary. An inquiry sent to the Rector of Al-Azhar university in Cairo in 1942 asked whether Jesus had ascended to heaven with his fleshly body and would come again with it in the last days. The shaikh replied that 'there is nothing in the Qur'ān, nor in the sacred traditions of the Prophet, which authorizes the correctness of the belief . . . that Jesus was taken up to the heaven with his body, and is alive there even now, and would descend therefrom in the latter days . . . Any person who denies his bodily ascent and his continuance in physical existence in the heavens, and his descent in the latter ages, does not deny a fact that can be established by clear conclusive arguments.'[1]

It is best to keep to the reserve of the Qur'ān and the Bible. Christians prefer the verse of the Bible which says, 'it is not for you to know about dates and times, which the Father has set within his own control'. (Acts 1,7) And for the future they would leave all things to God, and look for the consummation when Christ 'himself will also be made subordinate to God, who made all things subject to him, and thus God will be all in all'. (1 Cor. 15,28)

[1] *Islamic Review*, September 1961, pp. 11ff.

13

Son of God

It is now time to consider the Quranic and Biblical use of the word 'Son' as applied to Jesus. This seems to be one of the great points of difference between these holy books, yet perhaps the difference is not so great as appears at first sight. Some of 'the sects have differed', and the Qur'ān seeks to correct them.

There are many passages in the Qur'ān denying that God has offspring, and only a few can be quoted. Perhaps the most famous is the short sūra 112, al-Ikhlāṣ, the Unity: 'Say: "He is God, One; God, the eternal; he brought not forth, nor hath he been brought forth; Co-equal with him there hath never been any one".'

This short sura is one of the most popular, recited every day by most Muslims. It is a denial of God producing offspring in the human manner, and of God having any associates. It stresses the Unity of God and his difference from men. Since it is generally regarded as one of the earliest Meccan suras, this would mean that it was directed against the many gods of pagan Arabia, though later writers turned it also against Christian doctrine.

The attack on the polytheism of Mecca is taken up by name in 53,19–21: 'Have ye considered Al-Lāt, and Al-'Uzzā and the third, Manāt, the other (goddess)? Have ye male (issue) and he female?' This is a forceful rejection of the notion that God had either male or female offspring, and that the pagan gods or goddesses could be accommodated under this name. So constantly throughout the Qur'ān such pagan deities are rejected.

As W. M. Watt says, 'in passages denying that God has offspring the presumption is that the primary reference is to paganism unless there is a clear mention of Jesus'.[1]

What then is said about Jesus in this respect? There are only three clear references, apart from those which deal specifically with semi-trinitarian ideas which will be considered in the next chapter. The first is at the conclusion of the Meccan narrative of the birth of Jesus:

19,35–36/34–35: 'That is Jesus, son of Mary – a statement of the truth concerning which they are in doubt. It is not for God to take to himself any offspring; glory be to him! when he decides a thing, he simply says "Be!" and it is.'

This we saw earlier to be the declaration of the birth of Jesus by divine decree, rather than explaining it through vulgar biological speculation in the manner of the apocrypha. But for our present purpose the key words are 'take to himself any offspring'. 'Take to himself' means literally to 'acquire' (*yattakhidha*), and so this verse denies that God acquires a son in the course of time. This had been said by Adoptionist and Arian heretics in Christianity, who said that Jesus became or was adopted Son of God at his baptism or some other moment. But the orthodox rejected this in teaching that the Son is eternal (see next chapter).

There are many other Quranic verses that reject this notion of 'acquisition' of a son, usually with little clear reference to Christian or semi-Christian belief. So 10,69/68: 'They say, "God hath taken to himself offspring".' 25,2: 'To whom belongs the kingdom of the heavens and the earth, who hath not taken to himself offspring, and who hath never had any partner in the kingdom.' 19,93–94/91–93: 'They have attributed to the Merciful offspring, when it does not behoove the Merciful to take to himself offspring. There is no one in the heavens or in the earth but cometh to the Merciful as a servant.' 39,6/4: 'Should God wish to have offspring [or 'had God desired to take to him a son'], he would choose what he willeth of what he createth.'

[1] *Muhammad at Medina*, p. 318; see also his article 'Son' in *The Hibbert Journal*, 1950, pp. 245f., where pagan Arabian views of begetting gods are considered, and the Quranic words rendered, 'is it credible that God should have only daughters, when you Meccans have sons as well and consider daughters inferior?'

These may all be presumed to be directed primarily against pagan polytheism, or at the most against the Adoptionist heresy. But two other passages are more pointed. 4,169/171: 'The Messiah, Jesus, son of Mary, is only the messenger of God . . . God is only one God; glory be to him (far from) his having a son.' In the light of the above this can fairly be taken to mean that Jesus, as Messiah, was not added to God as a son.

Then 9,30 says: 'The Jews say that 'Uzair is the son of God, and the Christians say that the Messiah is the son of God; that is what they say with their mouths, conforming to what was formerly said by those who disbelieved; God fight them! how they are involved in lies! They take their scholars and monks as Lords apart from God, as well as the Messiah, son of Mary, though they were only commanded to serve one God, beside whom there is no other God; glory be to him above whatever they associate (with him)!'

'Uzair is the Biblical Ezra, the name being recognized by Muslim philologists as foreign. That he is here joined with the Messiah and with scholars and monks, suggests that saint-worship is in question. But the objection to the use of the word 'son' remains against the background of Arabian paganism, to which it 'could only mean one thing, namely, the son of God by cohabitation with a woman. That this is not what Christians meant by the term goes without saying.'[1]

What then do Christians, and in particular what does the Gospel, mean by the title 'Son of God'? In the Synoptic Gospels (Mark, Matthew, Luke) Jesus never speaks of himself as Son of God, and rarely, if ever, as Son. Cullmann speaks of Jesus' 'reserve' in using this title, and points out that his primary designation for himself was not 'Son of God' but 'Son of Man'.[2] 'Son of God' was said about Jesus by others, demoniacs, disciples, the high priest and the crowds at the cross. But Jesus himself clearly wished to avoid the misunderstandings that might be attached to this title, ideas that expressed wrong notions of the Messiah.

'Son' or 'Son of God' occur already in the Old Testament

[1] R. C. Zaehner, *At Sundry Times*, p. 203.

[2] *The Christology of the New Testament*, pp. 282, 290.

in a variety of ways, though not in any that suggest a physical begetting by God. 'Son' is used of the nation, 'I have called my son out of Egypt' (Hosea 11,1), and of the king, 'thou art my son, this day have I begotten thee'. (Psalm 2,7) It is used in the Old Testament apocrypha of the righteous, 'so shalt thou be as a son of the Most High'. (Sir. 4,10)

The title 'Son of Man' is found many times in all the Gospel sources, 'it is always used by Jesus, and not by others of him'.[1] There has been great discussion over the origins and meaning of this title, some saying that it means simply 'a man' or 'man in general', but it could also be used of the Messiah. While the title is used in a number of ways in the Old Testament, a crucial verse is Daniel 7,13: 'there came with the clouds of heaven one like unto a son of man', and this figure is later identified with 'the saints of the most High'. This figure apparently developed in the Old Testament apocrypha into a Messiah and his community, not merely an individual but a corporate vocation being seen in it. Jesus chose this title 'in conscious preference' to others. 'It expresses the idea of lordship, of rule over the Messianic community . . . Strange to the Gentile world, it embodies his conception of Messiahship.'[2] The Son of Man is the embodiment of the people of God, as in Daniel, seen in Jesus and his followers.

The term 'the Son' occurs in Mark (13,32), and in the stories of the baptism and the transfiguration and the parable of the wicked husbandmen, but not applied directly by Jesus to himself. Matthew and Luke add little to Mark's record, except in the important Son-Father passage: 'all things have been delivered unto me of my Father, and no one knoweth the Son except the Father; neither doth any know the Father, save the Son.' (Matt. 11,27; Lk. 10,22) This verse has been called 'a bolt from the Johannine blue', or 'part of a Christological hymn formed in a Hellenistic environment'.[3] It indicates the special position of the Messiah in the revelation and kingdom of God, and follows on his particular function that is sketched elsewhere in the Gospel. He reveals God, brings his kingdom, and in doing so is peculiarly close to him.

[1] *The Names of Jesus*, pp. 25ff. [2] *ibid.*, p. 35. [3] *ibid.*, pp. 62f.

The Gospel according to John uses the title Son of God most frequently, but also the 'only begotten Son', and especially 'the Son'. Paul also writes often of 'the Son of God', 'the Son', and 'his Son'. This usage by these two great theologians, John and Paul, shows Christianity moving out into the Greek world. On the other hand it is remarkable that 'Son' and 'Son of God' are not used at all in the Pastoral Epistles (Timothy and Titus) or in Peter and Jude, once in Revelation, and only twice in Acts.

The use of the word Father corresponds to that of Son, and needs consideration. In all the Gospels Jesus speaks of God as 'the Father' and 'my Father'. The original of this in Aramaic is preserved in one of his own prayers: 'Abba, father.' (Mk. 14,36) This is a development from the Old Testament which spoke of God as 'our father', but it is given a more individual note in the New Testament. Following the teaching and example of Jesus Christians have used and cherished the name Father for God. 'Our Father' is the commonest Christian prayer, going back to Christ himself. This has often been rejected by Muslims as describing God in too human a fashion, but Christians would claim that since the father-son relationship is the highest human bond it expresses most perfectly the bond between God and man. Other titles are used of God, King, Judge, Friend, and so on, but Father expresses his love most clearly. There are no sensual meanings attached to the names Father and Son, but they denote the grace and love of God to man, and the faith and love of man to God.

Some modern Muslim writers, instead of condemning the Christian use of the words Son and Father, have tried to understand them in their historical setting. Thus Sayyid Aḥmad Khān wrote: 'In the western world "father" is a term applied to the originator of something . . . the son is he whom God has formed with his hands . . . If we would express it in Arabic idiom, then "father" means *rabb* (Lord), and "son" *al-'abd al-maqbūl* (the chosen servant), and these meanings agree exactly with the application of these terms in the Old and New Testaments.' It may be debated whether in fact they do agree exactly with Biblical usage, but the intention to understand the Biblical terms can be appreciated. And on 'Son of God' he says:

'Amongst the Greeks it was commonly held that a very holy and reverenced person should be called "Son of God" ... When the disciples intended to spread the Christian religion by means of the Greek language they had to give Christ such a title of honour.'[1]

Other writers have made similarly conciliatory statements. In a Persian life of Jesus, by Shīn Parto, the Gospel story is accepted, including the true crucifixion and appearances after three days. This writer continues: 'The Christians say that he is Son of God, but it is better to call him Son of Love, one who was born in love, taught men love, and was crucified for love and liberty.' And the Egyptian Khālid M. Khālid quotes the Gospel titles 'Saviour of the world' and 'bread of life', speaks of God as 'Father', and says 'God is love'. Love is seen also by this writer as the chief characteristic of Jesus, love is the great law of the world, and his favourite Gospel saying is 'much has been forgiven, because she loved much'.[2]

K. Cragg, from the Christian side, has tried to show how the Christian usage of 'Son of God' can best be explained to Muslims, making an effort at conciliation and sympathetic interpretation such as has been rare until modern times. 'It is necessary in the Muslim context, though not in the Christian, to insist that the expression "Son of God" excludes all paternity in the physical sense. On Christian premises the latter is unthinkable. The phrase means that Christ is God in self-revelation, an activity which begets or generates a historic personality, wherein what God is in revelatory love, he is also known to be in revelatory action. The Father begets the Son in the sense that his "will" to reveal is translated into act. But all is of him and from him and by him.' And again, 'the terms "Father" and "Son" have no physical significance and are used analogically. The divine solicitude for man in ignorance and sin 'begets' or generates the activity of redeeming love which is evident in the historic Christ.'

A friendly critic of this statement went so far as to say that

[1] *Reforms and Religious Ideas of Sir Sayyid Aḥmad Khān*, pp. 80f.
[2] S. Parto, *Seven Faces*, Teheran; K. M. Khālid, *Together on the Road, Muhammad and Jesus*, Cairo.

'Muslims also admit the exalted position of Jesus, who saw with the eyes of God, talked with the tongue of God, and was absorbed (*fanā'*) in God, a position which is not incompatible with his not being God but remaining man, a very exalted man'.[1]

To Muslims belief in a Son of God seemed an offence against the unity of God, though there is a strange verse in sūra 43,81: 'Say: "If the All-Merciful has a son, then I am the first to serve him".' But to Christians the belief in Christ as 'Son' of God is 'the genesis and ground of our faith that the One Living and Eternal God has himself undertaken to tell men of himself'.[2] This leads directly to the idea of the Trinity.

[1] M. Hamidullah, in *The Islamic Quarterly*, 1956, review of *The Call of the Minaret*.
[2] K. Cragg, *The Call of the Minaret*, 1956, pp. 290f., 315. See also the suggestion that in Syriac apocrypha Son of God was virtually the equivalent of Apostle of God. G. Widengren, *Muḥammad, the Apostle of God*, p. 68.

14

Trinity

IT has often been thought that the Qur'ān denies the Christian teaching of the Trinity, and commentators have taken its words to be a rejection of orthodox Christian doctrine. However, it seems more likely that it is heretical doctrines that are denied in the Qur'ān, and orthodox Christians should agree with most of its statements. An examination of the different passages will show this.

5,19/17: 'Assuredly they have disbelieved who say that God is the Messiah, son of Mary.'

5,76/72: 'Assuredly they have disbelieved who say: "God is the Messiah, son of Mary".'

To say that God is Christ is a statement not found anywhere in the New Testament or in the Christian creeds. 'God was in Christ', said Paul, 'reconciling the world to himself'. (2 Cor. 5,19) But this reconciliation *through* Christ is quite different from saying that God *is* Christ. 'You belong to Christ, and Christ to God', said Paul again, putting the relationship into perspective. (1 Cor. 3,23)

But in the early Christian centuries there arose heresies, such as that of Patripassianism, which so identified Christ and God as to suggest that God the Father had suffered on the cross. About A.D. 200 Noetus had taught that Christ was God the Father, and therefore that the Father himself was born and suffered and died. These views were taken to Rome by Praxeas, of whom Tertullian said that 'he drove out prophecy and brought in heresy, he put to flight the Comforter and crucified the Father'.[1] The orthodox teaching of the Logos, the Word or 'Son' of God, was a defence against such heretical teaching, though it must be admitted that writers in later ages were not always careful enough in their use of these titles.

Sūra 5,77/73 then goes on to say: 'Assuredly they have disbelieved who say: "God is one of three" [or "the third of three"]. There is no god but one God.' The orthodox Christian must agree. God cannot be one of three. The notion of three gods is as offensive to Christianity as to Islam. Christianity claims to be monotheistic, to believe in one God only. The Nicene Creed begins, 'I believe in one God'. The Articles of the Church of England start with the affirmation: 'There is but one living and true God, everlasting, without body, parts, or passions; of infinite power, wisdom and goodness; the Maker and Preserver of all things both visible and invisible.'

Ibn Iṣhāq said that Christians of the Byzantine rite declared of Christ, 'he is the third person of the Trinity, which is the doctrine of Christianity . . . They argue that he is the third of three in that God says: We have done, We have commanded, We have created and We have decreed, and they say, If he were one he would have said I have done, I have created, and so on, but He is He and Jesus and Mary. Concerning all these assertions the Qur'ān came down.'[2] This may give the background for the next Quranic verse. 5,116 says: (Recall) when God said: 'O Jesus, son of Mary was it thou who didst say to the people: "Take me and my mother as two gods apart from God"? He replied: 'Glory be to thee! it is not for me to say what is not true; if I did say it, thou knowest it; thou knowest what is in my (inner) self.'

First of all Jesus is cleared of having suggested that he and Mary are two additional gods, or gods 'apart from God'. There is, of course, nothing in the Gospel to suggest that Jesus ever spoke in this fashion. The Qur'ān quotes his words, 'Serve God, my Lord and your Lord', which are in the Gospel even stronger, 'My Father and your Father, my God and your God'. (John 20,17)

Next, the exaltation of Mary as a god seems to be a reference

[1] See *Selections from Early Christian Writers*, p. 129.
[2] *The Life of Muhammad*, pp. 271f.

to heretical practice. Christian commentators have often seen in this verse an indication that the Trinity was conceived of as Father, Mother and Son, a divine family. But the Quranic verse need not mean that; it is a simple rebuttal of a practice that is repugnant to any monotheist.

The exaltation of Mary was a gradual process in Christian devotion. Although the apocryphal gospels came to speak of her 'perpetual' virginity, which the New Testament does not, yet the cult of Mary was slow in growing. To begin with she was not a martyr, and the veneration of the Christian martyrs was one of the most powerful motive forces of early devotion. Then there were pagan goddesses whose widespread worship repelled Christians from a cult that might seem like theirs. Paul had opposed Diana (or Artemis) of the Ephesians, but she continued to be worshipped for centuries. However, after the Nestorian controversy, in the fifth century, the title God-bearer or Mother of God came to be used widely, instead of the term Mother of Christ, and this was another stimulus to the cult of Mary. Festivals of Mary came to rival those of Christ, with both her birth and her ascension (assumption). However it was only as late as 1854 that the Roman Catholic church decreed the dogma of the Immaculate Conception of Mary, and in 1954 the corporal Assumption of Mary. But still in the Roman church Mary is officially regarded as a creature, and not as divine. The cult of Mary (hyperdulia) is distinguished in Roman Catholic teaching from the worship (latria) due to God alone.

In Arabia there were in the early centuries some (called Antidicomarianites) who protested against the idea of the perpetual virginity of Mary. But there were cults, some semi-pagan, which exalted Mary in unseemly fashion. The Collyridians, an Arabian female sect of the fourth century, offered to Mary cakes of bread (collyrida), as they had done to the great earth mother in pagan times. Epiphanius, who opposed this heresy, said that the Trinity must be worshipped, but Mary must not be worshipped. The Qur'ān may well be directed against this heresy. It gives its support against Mariolatry, while at the same time it recognizes the importance of Mary as the vessel chosen by God for the birth of his Christ.

The association of Mary and the Holy Spirit may also have been a factor in some interpretations of the Trinity. The Gospel according to the Hebrews already at an early date had spoken of 'my mother the Holy Spirit'. This occurred generally in quotations from the prophets (Isaiah, Jeremiah, Ezekiel), but according to Origen, writing in a Gospel commentary, the Gospel of the Hebrews said, 'The Saviour himself saith, "Even now my mother the Holy Spirit took me"'. And in the fourth century Aphraates of Edessa spoke of a man having God as his father and 'the Holy Spirit his Mother'.[1]

The Qur'ān also, here and in other verses, denounces the current pagan ideas of Mecca and Arabia of families of gods. Pagan deities were male and female and had children. We saw in the last chapter that it is probably here that lies the Muslim reluctance to use the term 'Son of God', because it might seem to imply physical procreation by God. This is in the Arabian context. But among the Jews, who were monotheists of long standing and had rooted out all fertility notions from their highly purified religion, the New Testament did not hesitate to speak of the Son of God, meaning the Messiah. Similarly, the Christian doctrine of the Trinity rigidly excludes all suggestions of physical generation, and any idea of polytheism or tritheism. God is one God, as Paul said, 'A false god has no existence in the real world. There is no God but one.' (1 Cor. 8,4)

It is in the light of the above that other Quranic references to 'three' gods may be understood. One of the most commonly quoted is 4,169/171: 'The Messiah, Jesus, son of Mary, is only

> the messenger of God, and his Word which he cast upon Mary, and a spirit from him. So believe in God and his messengers, and do not say: "Three". Refrain, (it will be) better for you; God is only one God; glory be to him (far from) his having a son!'

The interpretation, in the light of previous passages, would be: 'Do not say three gods.' And, 'Far from his acquiring a son' (in time, or by physical process).

Especially grave in Muslim eyes is *shirk*, 'association' of anyone with God, giving God a partner, and generally anything

[1] *The Apocryphal New Testament*, pp. 2f.; *Islam and Christian Theology*, i, p. 32.

that is in opposition to Quranic monotheism. *Shirk* is denounced in many verses of the Qur'ān. 5,76/72: 'Verily if anyone associates anything with God, God hath made the Garden inaccessible to him, and his resort is the Fire.' 9,31: 'One God, beside whom there is no other god; glory be to him above whatever they associate with him.' 7,190: 'Exalted by God (far) from what they associate (with him).' 16,53/51: 'God hath said: "Take not two gods"; he is simply one God.' 17,23/22: 'Set not up with God another god.' 17,111: 'Praise be to God who hath not taken to himself offspring, to whom there hath never been any partner in the sovereignty.' 19,36/35: 'It is not for God to take to himself any offspring.' 23,93/91: 'God hath not taken to himself any offspring, nor was there with him any (other) god.' 25/2: 'He, to whom belongs the kingdom of the heavens and the earth, who hath not taken to himself offspring, and who hath never had any partner in his kingdom . . . but they have taken for themselves apart from him gods who create nothing, being themselves created, who have not in their power hurt or profit to themselves, nor have they in their power death or life or raising to life.'

Most of this is clearly against Arabian polytheism, with an occasional warning to others against a similar error. In later writings the practisers of 'association' are often virtually identified with the unbeliever (*kāfir*), but in the Qur'ān *shirk* is used clearly of those who deny the unity of God.

The Qur'ān denies Christian heresies of Adoption, Patripassianism, and Mariolatry. But it affirms the Unity, which is at the basis of trinitarian doctrine. The Qur'ān, says R. C. Zaehner, 'does not explicitly *deny* any specific Christian doctrine except that Christ is the *son* of God, and this for obvious reasons that have already been pointed out. For, except to those well coached in Christian theology, sonship implies physical procreation and this is unthinkable in God who is a pure Spirit.'[1]

The perplexed reader may well ask, what then is the Christian teaching about the Trinity? As commonly expressed in western European languages this doctrine may give the appearance of tritheism. A recent writer says that 'from the point of view of

[1] *At Sundry Times*, p. 216.

religious devotion the tri-unity of God is spoken of in language which renders it indistinguishable from tritheism; but that God is other than one is a departure, if an unconscious one, from orthodoxy'.[1]

The official expression is 'three persons, in one God'. But the Latin *persona* meant a mask, and hence an aspect or revelation of God. The notion of 'aspects' had been expressed in the third century by Sabellius, who taught that Father, Son and Holy Spirit were one and the same, one God. But each was a character (*prosopon*) or form of manifestation of the one God, seen as Creator and Father, as Saviour and Son, and as present in the Spirit. Sabellian teaching was partly absorbed and partly rejected in the theology of the Nicene creed and later, from the fourth century onwards. The equality of the different 'aspects' or 'persons' was retained, but any suggestion of temporary 'modes' of deity was rejected. In some ways Sabellian teaching is the easiest to grasp, especially in the missions where other languages do not have the subtleties of Greek or Latin. One has heard the Trinity expounded in Africa as 'one God in three men', for the very word 'person' was lacking. To say, in these circumstances, 'one God in three powers' was nearer the orthodox creed.

K. Cragg says that, in interpreting their faith to Muslims, Christians 'must begin with this plea that the Muslim estimate and ponder the Christian Trinity, not as a violation of Unity, but as a form of its expression. We cannot proceed except on the understanding that we are both firmly and equally believers that God is One. We both stand squarely in the Hebrew tradition: "The Lord our Lord is ONE Lord". We are not discussing theism and tritheism. Christianity is concerned only with the first. Muslims who debate tritheism are not discussing Christianity. Where we differ is over how to define and understand the Divine Unity.'[2]

Christians hold that belief in the Trinity helps in understanding the Unity, indeed in safeguarding the Unity. In the Qur'ān God is not abstract and alone, he is in relationship with

[1] J. S. Bezzant, in *Objections to Christian Belief*, p. 103.
[2] *The Call of the Minaret*, p. 308.

men and he uses intermediaries to convey his messages to them. The very Qur'ān is thought of as the Word or Speech of God. God sends his angels and messengers to men, and he whispers his counsel to them. These show God at work in the world. God is creator. He is also revealer; in nature, in his messengers and in men. There is a kinship here with the Word and Spirit of Christian belief.

The Qur'ān speaks of God as creator. It also speaks of the Spirit (*rūḥ*) of God, and his Word (*kalima*) and Command (*amr*). 16,2 says: 'He sendeth down the angels with the Spirit from his affair (command, *amr*), to whomsoever he willeth of his servants.' 17,87/85 reads: 'They ask thee about the Spirit; say: "The Spirit belongs to my Lord's affair" ' (*amr*). It was suggested earlier (p. 51) that *amr* is akin to the Hebrew *memrā*, which corresponds to the Greek Logos, Word.[1] The Qur'ān also speaks several times of the 'Most Beautiful Names' of God (*al-asmā' al-ḥusnā*; 7,179/180; 17,110; 20,7/8; 59,24). These show the richness of the divine nature: 'He is God, the Creator, the Maker, the Former . . . the Sublime, the Wise.' 'Call upon Allah or call upon ar-Raḥmān; whichsoever ye call upon is entitled to the most beautiful names.' Later tradition and devotion was to dwell upon these and many other names.

Christian doctrine also has tried to expound this richness of the divine being and the divine manifestation, this diversity in unity. God as creator and provider is seen in the Father who cares for mankind. The essential nature of God as love manifesting himself in action is seen in the 'Son', in the humanity of Christ, his loving actions and words, his suffering and death. The ever-present nature of God is seen in the Spirit, who 'spoke by the prophets', in the light of other faiths, in the church, and in his power with us still. Yet these three are one, the threefold revelation of God to men.

When early Christians used the title 'Son' of God they meant to express the close relationship of Christ to God in the divine self-revelation. 'In him dwelt all the fulness [*pleroma*] of the godhead bodily', said Paul (Col. 2,9). This was because 'God was in Christ reconciling the world unto himself'. (2 Cor. 5,19) For

[1] *At Sundry Times*, p. 214.

devotion Christ became the expression of 'the invisible God', the manner in which the inapprehensible God became understood by men, so that the impersonal and infinite could be seen in a person. Devotion grasped this, though it did not always expound it clearly, but where it could not find adequate phrases it yet held on to the faith. When we speak of 'God the Son', says Cragg, 'we mean God in the act of revelation. When we speak of Beethoven the musician, or Leonardo da Vinci the artist, we mean these men in their full personality in particular capacity, capacities which do not preclude their having others, but yet involving them wholly.'[1] So God was revealed in his essential nature of love in Christ, but he is revealed in other ways in nature and in other faiths.

'A bare unity, philosophically understood, is a barren one . . . Entire transcendence is in the end a blank agnosticism. The Christian faith in the Holy Trinity only carries further the truth implicit in the Muslim faith in revelation and judgement. It is the Christian form of belief in a God who has real and meaningful relation with men and the temporal world.'[2]

A modern Muslim writer, commenting on these recent explanations of Christian faith, says: 'If such is the interpretation and conception of the doctrine of the Trinity, a Muslim finds hardly anything about which to differ from his Christian friends. The change of persons into attributes is nothing which is derogatory to the integral character of God. This new conception and interpretation is perhaps the re-echo of the beliefs of early Christian sects now extinct. It was Sabellius (A.D. 215) who maintained that Trinity was not a union of three persons but one Person, single Divine Essence, which manifested itself under three successive *aspects*, as Father, Son and Holy Spirit.'[3]

Other theologians might not accept this, but they would probably agree that the doctrines of the Trinity and the Person of Christ must be re-stated in modern terms, for they are partly unintelligible, and so irrelevant to modern thinking, as traditionally stated. 'Whatever the difficulties of the doctrine of the

[1] *The Call of the Minaret*, pp. 290f. [2] *ibid.*, p. 317.

[3] S. M. Tufail, in *Forum*, June 1960; see also H. A. Wolfson, 'Muslim Attributes and the Christian Trinity', in the *Harvard Theological Review*, 1956, pp. 1–18.

Tri-unity of God, at least it enables us, as was said long ago, to speak of personality *in* God rather than of the personality *of* God. No one has or can have exhaustive knowledge of God as he is in himself. Human personality may be, indeed must be, but a faint copy of Divine personality. The essential in theism is that God, as the ground of the universe, must be an intelligent and ethical being.'[1]

[1] *Objections to Christian Belief*, p. 106.

15

Gospel (Injīl)

THE revelations of God in the scriptures of other People of the Book are spoken of many times in the Qur'ān. The Jewish scriptures are referred to generally as the Taurāh, as the Jews themselves sometimes mean by Torah the whole of their Bible. But as the Pentateuch, the Torah in the first five books of the Old Testament, is more strictly the Law as revealed to Moses so in a few Quranic passages Taurāh seems to have the sense of Law. In 3,44/50 Jesus both confirms and enlarges the Torah: 'confirming what is before me of the Torah and that I may make allowable for you some things which have been forbidden to you.' All the references to the Torah are in Medinan passages, with the possible exception of 7,156/157 which speaks of the Torah and the Gospel mentioning the 'native' or 'illiterate' prophet who brought the revelation to a people who had no scriptures.

Mention is made three times of the *zabūr*, which in the singular is the book of David, the Psalter. Then there is reference to the Wisdom, *ḥikma*, which is given to prophets in the sense of a revealed book, but not identified with particular writings.

The word *Injīl* is always used for the Christian revelation, and particularly associated with Jesus. This word also occurs only in Medinan passages, with the exception of 7,156/157 which is traditionally regarded as late Meccan though it seems to have some Medinan references. The origins of *Injīl* are clearly the Greek εὐαγγέλιον, Evangel, Good News, Gospel (Old English god-spel). Whether it entered Arabic from Syriac or Ethiopic has been debated, but the Ethiopic *wangēl* has a long vowel like *Injīl* and this suggests that the word was brought over by Abyssinian Christians and it was probably in widespread use in Arabia before Muḥammad's time.[1]

Whether Injīl must be understood narrowly of the Gospel that Jesus preached, or more widely of the New Testament, the Christian scriptures, is a difficult question. Jesus brought the Gospel, but Christians later had the 'Injīl in their possession'. (7,156/157) This is a complex matter, and discussion must be deferred till later when consideration is given to the relationship between the words of Jesus and the four Gospels written by the evangelists, and the interdependence of the teaching and the life of Jesus.

The word Gospel (Injīl) occurs twelve times in the Qur'ān, as follows:

3,2/3: 'He sent down the Torah and the Gospel aforetime as guidance for the people.'

3,43/48: 'He will teach him the Book and the Wisdom and the Torah and the Gospel.'

3,58/65: 'Why do ye dispute about Abraham, seeing that the Torah and the Gospel were not sent down till after his time?'

5,50/46: 'We gave (Jesus) the Gospel, containing guidance and light, confirming the Torah which was before it, and as guidance and admonition to those who show piety.'

5,51/47: 'Let the people of the Gospel judge by what God hath sent down therein; if any do not judge by what God hath sent down, they are the reprobate.'

5,70/66: 'If they had established the Torah and the Gospel, and what has been sent down to them from their Lord, they would have eaten from above and from beneath their feet.'

5,72/68: 'O People of the Book, ye have nothing to stand upon until ye establish the Torah and the Gospel and what has been sent down to you from your Lord.'

5,109/110: 'I have taught thee the Book and the Wisdom and the Torah and the Gospel.'

7,156/157: 'The Gospel in their possession, urging them to what is reputable, and restraining them from what is disreputable,

[1] *The Foreign Vocabulary of the Qur'ān*, pp. 71, 95.

making good things allowable for them and foul things forbidden, relieving them of their burden and the shackles which have been upon them.'

9,112/111: 'A promise binding upon him in the Torah, the Gospel, and the Qur'ān.'

48,29: 'What they are compared to in the Gospel is a seed which puts forth its shoot.'

57,27: 'We gave (Jesus) the Gospel.'

In the Meccan sūra 19,31/30 comes the word attributed to Jesus: 'He hath bestowed on me the Book'. The above verses show that Jesus was given all the truths enshrined in the sacred books, the Torah and the Wisdom. Ibn Isḥāq said that 'in the Gospel is what Jesus brought in confirmation of Moses and the Torah he brought from God.'[1]

The holy books of Judaism, Christianity and Islam are seen as belonging to a sacred succession; they are not outdated, but all bring divine truth to give guidance to men. Sūra 3,2/3, addressed to Muḥammad, says: 'He hath sent down to thee the Book with the truth, confirming what was before it, and he sent down the Torah and the Gospel aforetime as guidance for the people, and he sent down the Furqān'. The Furqān is 'discrimination' or 'revelation'. According to Zamakhsharī it is used of the whole class of heavenly books, as in 21,49/48: 'We gave to Moses and Aaron the Furqān and illumination.' But in 3,2/3 and 25,1 and elsewhere it seems to be used of the Qur'ān: 'Blessed be he who hath sent down the Furqān upon his servant.' In this sense the Qur'ān is the Furqān as discrimination or criterion of truth, to make clear what went before. It is not an abrogation of previous scriptures, but a confirmation and a touchstone of truth, making clear what they meant: 'This Qur'ān is not such as to have been invented apart from God; but it is a confirmation of what is before it, and a distinct setting forth of the Book in which there is no doubt, from the Lord of the worlds.' So also 2,91/97: 'Gabriel – verily he hath brought it down upon thy heart with the permission of God confirming what was before it.'

If there was difficulty about the Qur'ān then the previous

[1] *The Life of Muhammad*, p. 258.

books should be referred to. So Muḥammad is told: 'If thou art in doubt as to what we have sent down to thee, ask those who recite the Book before thee.' (10,94) On the other hand the Qur'ān clears up previous doubts: 'Verily this Qur'ān recounts to the Children of Israel most of that in regard to which they differ.' (27,78/76) As there are different messengers, so the message comes in different ways. The Arabs had no scriptures in their own language: 'Thus have we sent it down an Arabic code . . . for every term there is a book.' (13,37/38) Here was shown the special purpose of warning Mecca and Medina: 'Thus have we suggested to thee an Arabic Qur'ān in order that thou mayest warn the mother of the towns.' (42,5/7)

Behind the written books is the heavenly original or archetype, the 'Mother of the Book' (*umm al-kitāb*). 'Lo it is in the Mother of the Book in our presence, exalted, wise.' (43,3/4; 3,5/7; 13,39) And again: 'A messenger from God reciting sheets kept pure, in which are Books true.' (98,2) Messengers may be thought of as receiving books from God, copies of the heavenly original, as some of the apocryphal epistles said that Jesus had a book which he revealed to his disciples.[1]

There is no suggestion in the Qur'ān that the Gospel given to Jesus was different from the canonical Gospels held by Christians. This is a matter of importance, in view of later Muslim polemic. Indeed the Qur'ān enjoins the 'people of the Gospel' to 'judge by what God hath sent down therein'. (5,51/47) It speaks of 'the Gospel in their possession' (7,156/157) and urges them to follow the messenger spoken of in it. The Qur'ān itself is sent down to confirm the Book which was before it, and to act as a 'protector over it'. (5,52/48)

However, the Qur'ān notes that there were differences of interpretation of both Torah and Gospel. 'We bestowed upon the Children of Israel the book . . . they did not differ till after the knowledge had come to them, out of mutual jealousy; verily thy Lord will decide between them on the day of resurrection in regard to the things in which they have been differing.' (45,15f./16f.) There was misunderstanding of the Gospel also, not because of defect in the sacred book, but through

[1] H. J. Bardsley, *Reconstructions of Early Christian Documents*, pp. 32, 334.

human sin; 'the sects disagreed among themselves'. (19,38/37) So Ibn Isḥāq said: 'He sent down the Criterion, i.e. the distinction between truth and falsehood about which the sects differ in regard to the nature of Jesus and other matters.'[1]

It is not certain when the Gospel was first translated into Arabic. A Monophysite scholar Johannes is said to have made a translation between A.D. 631 and 640, by order of an Arab prince. But the oldest Arabic fragments that survive of translations of the Gospels date from the ninth century. However, portions of the Gospels may have circulated in Arabia earlier and George, bishop of Arab tribes in Mesopotamia, wrote comments on the Bible about 570. It was noted in chapter 10 that Ibn Isḥāq's reference to the Comforter is taken from the Palestinian Syriac. It seems that Christian teaching in the sixth century A.D. was done in Arabia by oral versions of the scriptures, or from Syriac and Ethiopic texts.[2]

Later Muslim writers spoke of the 'corruption' (*taḥrīf*) of the scriptures by Jews and Christians. The Ebionites, Judeo-Christians, had already accused the Jews of corrupting their scriptures. Muslim writers differed in their opinions about what had been done. Some scholars (e.g. Bīrūnī) declared that Jews and Christians had actually altered the text of the Bible. But others (Ṭabarī, Ibn Khaldūn, etc.) said that they had interpreted the words incorrectly. It was argued that *taḥrīf* meant to change a thing from its original nature, but no man could possibly corrupt words that came from God. So at the most Christians could only corrupt by misrepresenting the meaning of the word of God. Muslims could do the same with the Qur'ān and Jews with the Torah. The Gospel was in its original purity, but it was possible to distort its meaning by unsound arguments. This was the teaching of Bukhārī, and sura 3,72/78 was quoted to show that the Jews might misinterpret the scriptures yet these remained intact: 'A part of them twist their tongues in the Book, that ye may think it to be a bit of the Book, though it is not a bit of the Book . . . Be ye rabbis in virtue of your teaching the Book, and in virtue of your having studied it.'

In modern times some popular polemic may blame Christians

[1] *The Life of Muhammad*, p. 272. [2] *Encyclopaedia of Islam*, art. Injīl.

for corrupting the Gospel, yet there are Muslim commentators who prefer the view that exposition has been at fault rather than any tampering with the text. Sayyid Aḥmad Khān, who wrote the first commentary on the Bible by a Muslim, followed this viewpoint and he tried to bring Christian and Muslim exegesis into agreement. Another writer says: 'In the Koran *taḥrīf* means either false interpretation of the passages bearing upon Mohammed or non-enforcement of the explicit laws of the Pentateuch. As for the text of the Bible, it had not been altered . . . No rival text is assumed.'[1]

There remains the difficult problem of the relationship between the Gospel, the Good News that Jesus taught, and the record of his words in the four Gospels. There is no evidence that Jesus ever wrote a line of his teaching. Muslims also believe that Muḥammad was illiterate and hence the written Qur'ān was recorded by his followers; secretaries like Zaid ibn Thābit collected the written and oral fragments from 'scraps of parchment and leather, tablets of stone, ribs of palm branches, camels' shoulder-blades and ribs, pieces of board, and the breasts of men'. A similar process took place with the Gospel, though it had long been written down by the time of Muḥammad. The canonical Gospels had been separated by the church from apocryphal legends. The first evangelists collected their material, as Luke says, from eyewitnesses and ministers of the word, and they tried to trace 'the course of all things accurately from the first'. (Lk. 1,2f.)

Yet one difference between the Qur'ān and the Bible remains in that the latter is not simply teaching but also narrative, and written from varying points of view. K. Cragg has shown what an obstacle this makes to the Muslim who opens the Christian scriptures. 'The Muslim who addresses himself to the Bible finds a variety of books of independent authorship, stretching over more than a millenium . . . It is difficult to comprehend why there should be four Gospels, when the Gospel, or Injīl, entrusted by God to Jesus the Prophet was reputedly a single book. The assumption is that because there are four, none of

[1] *The Reforms and Religious Ideas of Sir Sayyid Aḥmad Khān*, p. 78; M. H. Ananikian, in *The Moslem World*, xiv, pp. 61ff.

them is valid.' Cragg goes on to agree that many words of Jesus are 'irretrievably lost', but so also are many of the casual words and conversations of Muḥammad from the course of his long life. The question is whether any vital message has been lost, and what there is that makes the message more than words but also a life lived.[1]

A Muslim writer asks, 'Since Jesus did not dictate his teachings and have them written down, what guarantee is there of exact reporting in the biographies which constitute the present Gospels?' He says that they resemble neither Qur'ān nor Ḥadīth, but the books of Sīra, they are biographies. And he goes on to ask whether the Aramaic original in which Jesus spoke was preserved, why four Gospels were chosen, why there are internal differences if they were inspired by God, and whether all manuscripts are the same.[2]

Muslim writers today are aware of the work of textual critics of the Bible over the last century, and some assume that this means that the scriptures are unreliable. 'Not understanding the demand for utter scientific liberty behind such studies, the average Muslim conversant with them assumes that quite evidently even Christians are at sea over their scriptures.'[3] The scientific study of the Gospels has revealed in fact that they are not just biographies but preaching (*kerygma*), a message about Jesus as the Christ of God.

Others seem to want to have it both ways. Thus Yusuf 'Alī says that 'the Injīl spoken of by the Qur'ān is not the New Testament. It is not the four Gospels now received as canonical. It is the single Gospel which, Islam teaches, was revealed to Jesus, and which he taught. Fragments of it survive in the received canonical Gospels and in some others of which traces survive.' Rather unfortunately he cites the apocryphal infancy 'Gospels' and the very late so-called Gospel of Barnabas. 'Alī then goes on to say, however, that 'Muslims are therefore right in respecting the present Bible (New Testament and Old Testament), though they reject the peculiar doctrines taught by orthodox Christianity and Judaism'.[4]

[1] *The Call of the Minaret*, pp. 275ff.
[2] M. Hamidullah, in *The Islamic Quarterly*, 1956, review of the above.
[3] *The Call of the Minaret*, loc. cit.
[4] *Commentary on the Qur'ān*, p. 287.

W. C. Smith, from the Christian side, has also said that the identification of the Gospels with the Injīl 'cannot but be regarded as an error by Christians and by historians of religion, one that has caused some Christians to smile and others to protest'. He proceeds to draw a careful distinction between the revelation itself and the record of revelation. The Bible is only the latter, and he compares the Gospels with Tradition rather than with the identical words of Jesus. 'The parallel between the New Testament, and especially the four Gospels, and Ḥadīth, is seen to be quite close as soon as one thinks about it. For Moslems to say that Jesus brought the Injīl is as though Christians were to say of Muḥammad that he brought the Traditions.'[1]

Perhaps it is more correct to say that Jesus brought the Injīl, the Good News which he preached, but that the Gospels are more than that Injīl. They both include it and go beyond it. The Christian Gospels reveal not only the words of Jesus but his activity. These are mediated through the various versions of the men upon whom the essence of the works and words of Christ were indelibly impressed. 'On the Christian view it is not only comprehensible, it is desirable, that the significance of that Life and Death should be recorded as it impressed itself upon minds within the Church. The Gospels bring a cumulative witness to a central Figure without conspiring to eliminate secondary divergencies ... They exist ... to report his significance – words and deeds – as a glorious possession.'[2]

So K. Cragg urges the study of the Bible, which has been too often 'a treasure unexplored because it is thought of as possessed. It is a prisoner who cannot state his case because it is thought to have been already decided. In this situation, the Christian must rely on the inherent worth of the Scriptures and press for a new attention to their contents.' For in the Gospel the figure of Jesus comes in full light; 'the stirring words, the deep insights, the gracious deeds, the compelling qualities of him who was called the Master ... Is the Sermon on the

[1] 'Some Similarities and Differences between Christianity and Islam', in *The World of Islam*, 1959, pp. 52f.
[2] *The Call of the Minaret*, pp. 261f., 275f.

Mount to be left in silence in the Muslim's world? Must the story of the Good Samaritan never be told there? the simple, human story of the prodigal son never mirror there the essence of waywardness and forgiveness?'[1]

Happily the studies now being made of the life of Jesus in the Muslim world show that the Gospels are being read for their own sake, and with fairness and understanding. Professor Ḥusaini has said that 'the favourable attitude of the Qur'ān towards Christ and Christianity has determined the attitude of modern Muslim writers, whose sympathy and love for Christ are diffused through all their works'. And he continues by speaking of the 'full compatibility' of New Testament and Qur'ān in their faith, if not in the interpretations that have been given to their words.[2]

The growing knowledge of the Bible among Muslims, and the interest in the life and teaching of Jesus, have led to careful study of the text of the Gospels. Those who follow the movements of 'back to the Qur'ān' or 'people of the Qur'ān' have also been led to avoid the distortions of commentators and to note the reverent attitude of the Qur'ān towards Jesus. At the same time Western scholars have tried to make impartial studies of the Qur'ān and respectful appreciations of the Prophet Muḥammad. Only good can come from reverential understanding of each other's holy writings.

This is in line with the teaching of the Qur'ān which urged belief in the Bible: 'We have believed in God and what has been sent down to Abraham . . . and what has been given to Moses and Jesus.' (2,130/136) So men are urged to follow the Bible: 'O People of the Book, ye have nothing to stand upon until ye establish the Torah and the Gospel and what has been sent down to you from your Lord.' (5,72/68) On this Professor Ḥusaini remarks that 'it is evident from the Qur'ān that Islam did not abrogate the religions which preceded it. On the contrary, it enjoined all believers: Jews, Christians and Sabaeans, to follow their scriptures.'

[1] *The Call of the Minaret*, pp. 261f.

[2] *The Muslim World*, l, p. 302; see also 'The Attitude of Islam towards other religions', in *Internationaler Kongress für Religionsgeschichte*, X, 1961, pp. 153f.

The Gospels then truly contain the word of God to men, given by Christ who is the 'Word from God himself' (3,40/45), to whom God gave the Gospel. The Gospel still 'contains guidance and light', and it both confirms the Torah and gives 'admonition to those who show piety'. (5,50/46) The revelation given to Muḥammad and to Muslims came to 'confirm the Book which was before it', and to act 'as a protector over it'. (5,52/48)

16

Christians (Naṣārā)

Christians are honoured in several verses of the Qur'ān, but their sectarian differences are criticized, and monasticism is viewed with suspicion when corrupted.

The name Naṣārā for Christians is used regularly in the Qur'ān, and has remained in currency among Muslims down to this day, though other titles are now also used ('Īsawī or Maṣīḥī, followers of Jesus or the Christ). It seems clear that Naṣārā was used in pre-Islamic times, since sūra 5,85/82 speaks of those who say 'We are Naṣārā'. Indeed the word occurs in early Arabic poetry. The Mandaeans also called themselves Naṣārī, but this was in Islamic times and probably to escape persecution since Christians might be protected as People of the Book. A similar word, Naṣsurai, in early Mandaean manuscripts refers rather to practitioners of magic, and the Mandaeans call Christians Mshihiia, followers of the Messiah.[1]

It is probable that Naṣārā came from Syriac and originated from the title Nazarene. It is curious, however, that although Jesus was called Nazarene, or 'of Nazareth' (Nazōraios), a number of times, the title Nazarene is only given to Christians once in the New Testament (Acts 24,5). It was specifically Jewish, whereas the name that came to be popular, Christian, was especially Gentile as the religion moved out into the larger world. There was a Jewish-Christian sect known as Nazaraeans, which used the Gospel according to the Hebrews. However, in

[1] E. S. Drower, *The Mandaeans of Iraq and Iran*, p. 4; *Foreign Vocabulary of the Qur'ān*, p. 280.

Syriac, Christians were called Naṣrāyé, and this spread into parts of the eastern empires and was applied exclusively to Christians.[1]

In the Qur'ān Naṣārā seems to apply to all kinds of Christians, Byzantine, Nestorian and Monophysite. It occurs only in Medinan passages, and this, together with the fact that Injīl occurs chiefly in these suras, suggests that it was not until the Prophet moved to Medina that many messages came concerning Christians.

Naṣārā is used fifteen times in the Qur'ān, and in fourteen of them in association with the Jews as well. There are many other references to the People of the Book, too numerous to mention. Most of these may refer to Jews, but some to Christians also. We shall consider those that mention the Naṣārā by name. Reference was made in chapter 10 to the name *ḥawārīyūn*, 'apostles', for the followers of Jesus. Also the fact that they are called 'helpers' (*anṣār*) may have a link with the title Naṣārā (see p. 94 above).

2,59/62: 'Those who have believed, those who have judaised, the Naṣārā and the Ṣābi'īn, whoever has believed in God and the Last Day, and has acted uprightly, have their reward with their Lord; fear rests not upon them, nor do they grieve.'

This is a characteristic statement, recognizing that all who truly believe in God, Jews, Christians, and others will be rewarded on the Last Day. Who the Sabaeans were is not clear, the name has been interpreted as 'honoured' or 'baptizers' (see p. 59). Some writers have identified them with the Mandaeans, while others think they were a distinct pagan sect at Ḥarrān in Mesopotamia. Even the latter may have had parts of common belief with the Mandaeans. Since the Qur'ān names them along with People of the Book, and honours them, the assumption is that they were monotheists.[2]

5,73/69 says exactly the same. 22,17 repeats it with slight differences, including the Magians (*majūs*, Zoroastrians) who were monotheists, and the Polytheists who will be 'distinguished': 'Those who have believed, those who have judaised, the

[1] A. Mingana, *Syriac Influence on the Style of the Kur'ān*, p. 22.
[2] *The Mandaeans of Iraq and Iran*, p. xvi.

Ṣābi'īn, the Naṣārā, the Magians, and the Polytheists – verily God will distinguish between them on the day of resurrection.'

These passages recognize the worth of other religions, if they had scriptures and believed in one God. They have been valuable in inculcating tolerance among Muslims in the past, and in modern times they have guided thought and action in the closer relationships that now obtain between all religions.

Soon, however, the differences of Jews and Christians came into sight, their disputes and exclusiveness:

2,105/107: 'They say: "No one but those who are Jews or Christians will enter the Garden" . . . The Jews say: "The Christians have no ground to stand on", and the Christians say: "The Jews have no ground to stand on"; though they both recite the Book. So also those who have no knowledge say much the same. God will judge between them on the Day of Resurrection in regard to that in which they have been differing.'

The refusal of some Jews and Christians to admit the prophetic inspiration of Muḥammad is countered by an appeal to the guidance of God, and some did believe. 2,114f./120f.: 'Neither the Jews nor the Christians will be satisfied with thee until thou followest their creed; say: "The guidance of God is the guidance" . . . Those to whom we have given the Book and who recite it as it should be recited – they believe in it; those who disbelieve in it – they are the losers.' On this a modern Muslim commentator remarks that Muslims are the true Christians since they follow, or should follow, the teaching of Christ while rejecting later doctrines about him.

Before long the appeal to Jews and Christians is made on further grounds still:

2,129/135: 'They say: "Be ye Jews or Christians, and ye will be guided". Say (thou): "Nay, the creed of Abraham, who was a Ḥanīf, but was not one of the idolaters".'

2,134/140: 'Or do ye say "Abraham and Ishmael and Isaac and Jacob and the Patriarchs were Jews or Christians?"'

And with this may be included 3,60f./67f.: 'Abraham was not a Jew, nor was he a Christian, but he was a Ḥanīf, a Muslim, and he was not one of the Polytheists. Surely the people who are nearest to Abraham are those who followed him, and this prophet and those who have believed; God is the patron of the believers.'

These passages show that Muslims, like Jews and Christians, are in the succession of Abraham, being men of faith in God. The word *ḥanīf* occurs in late Meccan and Medinan passages, and may have come from Syriac usage by Christians for those who were neither Jews nor of their own faith. In the Qur'ān it is the name given to those who possess the true religion, and is particularly used of Abraham in contrast with pagan idolaters. Abraham was the father of true believers before the coming of Judaism or the Torah.

Christian apologists argued already that Abraham's faith was counted to him for righteousness in the heathen times before Judaism. Paul had taught that Abraham received 'a seal of the righteousness of the faith which he had while he was yet in uncircumcision'. (Rom. 4,11) Against Jewish exclusiveness, which would restrict its religion to the physical children of Abraham, Paul declared that the true children of Abraham were any who had his faith, irrespective of race or ancestry: 'They which are of faith, the same are sons of Abraham. And the scripture, foreseeing that God would justify the Gentiles by faith, preached the Gospel beforehand unto Abraham, saying, "In thee shall all the nations be blessed". So then they which are of faith, are blessed with faithful Abraham.' (Gal. 3,7f.)

It cannot be denied, of course, that Abraham was neither Jew nor Christian. The Jews, strictly, were members of the tribe of Judah who was Abraham's great-grandson. As a separate kingdom Judah emerged after the division of the monarchy at Solomon's death, and became the sole kingdom after the fall of Samaria in 722 B.C. 'Judaism', as a religion, is generally spoken of only after the exile, from 538 B.C. onwards or even after Christian times.

At a deeper level, these Quranic verses are a criticism of the exclusivism of Judaism and Christianity. They were unwilling to accept Muḥammad as prophet. They were divided amongst themselves, each sect thinking it had the truth and anathematizing the others. From this they were recalled to faith in God and the teaching of their own scriptures.

This is taken up again in sūra 5, where both Jews and Christians are reminded of the covenants that God made with them, the unfaithful are warned, and the sects are rebuked.

5,15–17/12–13: 'God made a covenant with the Children of Israel . . . With those also who say: "We are Naṣārā", we made a covenant, but they have forgotten part of the reminder given them; so we have stirred up enmity and hatred amongst them until the day of resurrection, and in the end God will announce to them what they have been doing.'

Then Jews and Christians are warned against presumption, and physical sonship from God is excluded (see our earlier chapter on Son of God).

5,21/18: 'The Jews and the Christians say: "We are the sons and beloved of God"; say: "Why then does he punish you for your sins? Nay, ye are human beings (part) of those whom he hath created; he forgiveth whom he pleaseth and punisheth whom he pleaseth".'

The exclusiveness of Jews and Christians brings the sad statement in 5,56/51: 'O ye who have believed, do not choose Jews and Christians as friends; they are friends to each other; whoever makes friends of them is one of them.'

But this is not the final word, indeed it is qualified by following verses. We have seen above that 5,73/69 is one of the verses which says that there is no fear upon the Jews and Christians that act uprightly. Then 5,85/82 discriminates between Jews and Christians, and shows the latter to have been more sympathetic to the message of Muḥammad. 3,48/55 had already said, to Jesus, 'I am going to set those who have followed thee above those who have disbelieved until the day of resurrection'.

4,157/159 said: 'There is no People of the Book but will surely believe in him before his death.' Then the Qur'ān goes even further, addressing Muslims:

5,85f./82f.: 'Assuredly thou wilt find . . . those of them who are nearest in love to those who have believed to be those who say: "We are Naṣārā"; that is because there are among them priests and monks, and because they count not themselves great. When they hear what has been sent down to the messenger, one sees their eyes overflowing with tears because of the truth which they recognize; they say: "O our Lord, we believe, so write us down among those who bear witness. Why should we not believe in God and the truth which has come down to us, and crave that our Lord should cause us to enter with the upright folk?" '

This is the first mention of the Christian monk (*rāhib*), though both solitaries and monastic communities were known to the pre-Islamic Arabs. Christians are 'nearest in love' to Muslims, and monks and priests are kindly people. But the monk and the priest (*qissīs*) were liable to corruption, and to the special dangers of pride and wealth which came through the veneration in which they were held and the gifts that would be bestowed upon them. This is indicated in the next reference:

9,30–34: 'The Jews say that 'Uzair is the son of God, and the Christians say that the Messiah is the son of God . . . They take their scholars and monks as lords apart from God . . . many of the scholars and monks consume the wealth of the people in vanity.'

The Biblical meaning of the word 'son', as non-physical when applied to Jesus has been explained earlier. There may be a reference to saint cults also here, and it is well known that legends and devotions grew up around the lives of some of the Christian martyrs and ascetics.

Apart from 22,17, listed above, that is the end of the mentions of Naṣārā by name. But, in addition to the many words about the People of the Book, some referring to Jews and some to Christians, there is a specific and kindly word about monks and others later:

57,27: 'Jesus, son of Mary . . . We set in the hearts of his followers kindness and mercy, and monasticism – they invented it, we did not prescribe it for them, except (it arose) out of desire for the satisfaction of God; but then they did not tend it as it ought to have been tended; those of them who believed we have given their reward, but many of them are reprobate.'

There have been different interpretations of this passage. The older version, given by Rāzī, takes the object of the words 'we set in their hearts' to be 'kindness, mercy and monasticism'. He adds that the Christians instituted this, and made it a pious but not obligatory practice. It arose 'out of desire for the satisfaction of God'; though 'they did not tend it as it ought to have been tended'. Later commentators separated 'monasticism' from the two other virtues set in their hearts and insisted that God had not prescribed it. This joined up with the Tradition that there must be 'no monkery in Islam'. But this tradition does not occur in the older canonical collections of Ḥadīth. Monkery or monasticism (*rahbānīya*) is only mentioned here (57,27) in the Qur'ān, and it is spoken of in a kindly, though perhaps critical, way.

There may be a further reference to monastic groups, or perhaps to a Jewish clan, in 3,109f./113f.: 'They are not all alike; there is a community of the People of the Book which is steadfast reciting the signs of God and at the drawing on of night, prostrating themselves, believing in God and the Last Day, urging what is reputable and restraining from what is disreputable, and vying in good deeds; these are the upright'.

But some of the most moving verses of the Qur'ān, which have often been taken to use the symbolism of Christian churches or monasteries the light of whose worship reflected that of God, are in sura 24,35–37:

'God is the light of the heavens and the earth;
His light is like a niche in which is a lamp,
the lamp in glass and the glass like a brilliant star,
lit from a blessed tree, an olive neither of the East nor of the West,
whose oil would almost give light even though no fire did touch it;
Light upon light;
God guideth to his light whomsoever he willeth . . .'

Bell comments that the rhymes, 35a originally joined to 36,37, confirm Macdonald's suggestion that a lighted altar of a Christian church is in mind, and there is a canonical variation to suggest some rearrangement of the lines. To travellers in Arabian caravans distant churches must often have shone like this; and in a later verse (39) the unbelievers are compared to a mirage in the desert. The 'niche' recalls a saying given by Ibn Isḥāq from the emperor of Abyssinia; 'This (message of Muḥammad) and what Jesus brought have come from the same niche'. It is a lamp niche (*mishkāt*) that is meant, such as were seen in churches, and in Arab legend light was miraculously manifested about saints or their tombs.[1] Places of worship are clearly in mind in the following verses, and if the first part of verse 35 was joined up with 36 the light in the niche is more clearly that of religious oratories:

> 'In houses which God hath permitted to be raised and his name to be remembered therein;
> In which give glory to him in the mornings and the evenings,
> Men whom neither trade nor bargaining divert from the remembrance of God . . .
> Each one knoweth his prayer and his giving of glory, and God knoweth what they do.'

In sūra 18 the famous story of the Seven Sleepers or People of the Cave (Aṣḥāb al-Kahf) is related, and a few modern commentators have taken this to be directed against Christians. But this is clearly not so. They are not mentioned by name, and only those are warned who say, 'God hath taken to himself offspring'. It has been seen that this notion of acquisition of offspring is not orthodox Christianity. But, further, the Seven Sleepers were in fact Christian martyrs, young men who were walled up alive during the harsh and widespread persecutions by the emperor Decius in A.D. 250. Their cave and the sanctuary built over it at Ephesus are mentioned by historians from A.D. 550, and it still remains a place of pilgrimage. To this the Qur'ān refers, 'Erect over them a building'. (18,20/21) The details were in dispute, some said there were three youths, some five, some seven and a dog, 'My Lord knoweth their number

[1] *The Life of Muhammad*, p. 152; see review of this by R. B. Serjeant in *Bulletin of the School of Oriental and African Studies*, 1958.

best'. They were said to remain in the cave over three hundred years, which number was later interpreted mystically, or more prosaically made to correspond with the length of time of all the Roman persecutions. Later Islam venerated these martyrs; some said the first trumpet of the Judgement would sound in the cave at Ephesus, others that the Seven Sleepers would go with the Messiah to the capture of Jerusalem and would die martyrs. Still today sura 18, the Cave, is recited as preliminary to the great Friday midday prayer throughout the Muslim world, and is broadcast on the radio as well. This shows the recognition that the Qur'ān honours these young martyrs, who confessed God and refused to call on any other god: 'They were young men who believed in their Lord, and we increased them in guidance.' (18,12/13)[1]

Many different attitudes were taken up in later Islamic days towards Christians, but it is worth saying something of the relationships of Muḥammad with them; they were much more friendly than his relationships with Jews, especially towards the end. C. C. Torrey has tried to show that Muḥammad's knowledge of Christianity came from Jews rather than Christians, though his statements are questionable. He speaks of one of Muḥammad's acquaintances who seems to have come from Persia or Babylon, 'he was certainly a learned man, probably a Jew, certainly *not* a Christian. The passage in which he is mentioned (16,105/103) is late Meccan'. He says that this Jew, like some others, respected Jesus but rejected Christian dogma. 'Any vilification of Jesus' would have led Muḥammad to oppose his ideas, but Muḥammad adopted this Jewish attitude to Jesus.[2]

The passage in question must be quoted: 'We know pretty well that they say: "It is only a human being who teaches him"; the speech of him they hint at is foreign; but this is Arabic speech clear.' (16,105/103)

But Ibn Isḥāq said plainly that the man in question here was a Christian. 'According to my information the apostle used often to sit at al-Marwa at the booth of a young Christian called Jabr, a slave of the B. al-Ḥaḍramī, and they used to say, "The

[1] L. Massignon, *Les Sept Dormants d'Ephèse en Islam et en Chrétienté*, 1955, pp. 62ff.
[2] C. C. Torrey, *The Jewish Foundation of Islam*, 1933, p. 74f.

one who teaches Muḥammad most of what he brings is Jabr the Christian, slave of the B. al-Ḥaḍramī". Then God revealed in reference to their words, "We know well that they say, 'Only a mortal teaches him' ". The tongue of him at whom they hint is foreign, and this is a clear Arabic tongue.'[1]

Baiḍāwī and other commentators mentioned this Christian Jabr and another Yasāra, and the Traditions related that Muḥammad used to stop and listen to these two Christians as they read aloud the Torah and the Gospel; this is recorded by Ḥusain. Yasāra, also called Abū Fukaiha, is said to have suffered much persecution; his daughter married a Muslim convert, Hattab, who was one of the refugees to Abyssinia. It is possible that both Jabr and Yasāra were Abyssinian slaves, and the name Jabr may be an Arabic version of Gabrū meaning 'slave' in Ethiopic. If this is so then the tongue of these men would indeed be 'foreign', and they would no doubt read the Gospel in Ethiopic. We saw in the last chapter that there was probably no translation of the Gospel in Arabic in the time of Muḥammad.

Khadīja, wife of Muḥammad, had a cousin called Waraqa who was one of those Meccans who had broken with polytheism before Islam and became a Christian. Waraqa had studied the Christian scriptures till he mastered them and was regarded as a scholar. He had written down the Gospels in Hebrew. He was old and said to be weary of waiting for a prophet or religious revelation. When Khadīja told him that Muḥammad had been hailed by a monk as a prophet, and that the monk had seen two angels shading him, he said, 'If this is true, Muḥammad is the prophet of this people'. After the call of Muḥammad to prophecy, and the vision of Gabriel, the Prophet told Khadīja what he had seen, and she rose up to tell Waraqa. Waraqa said, both to Khadīja and later to Muḥammad, that the greatest Nāmūs (angel Gabriel or heavenly Law) had come to him, and he was the prophet of this people. He foretold persecution and promised his support, but he died a few years later.[2]

The Prophet knew a number of other individual Christians.

[1] *The Life of Muhammad*, p. 180.

[2] *ibid.*, pp. 83, 99, 107. Nāmūs is the Syriac 'law', from Greek *nomos* (νόμος).

Salmān the Persian had been a Zoroastrian and keeper of the sacred fire, and then a Christian who had lived for years with monks and bishops. He recognized Muḥammad as prophet, though since he was a slave he was only able to join him later at Medina after Muḥammad had helped pay his ransom.[1] Of more interest is Zaid b. Ḥāritha, so close to the Prophet, who came from parents belonging to Christian tribes in the south of Syria. He was bought by Khadīja and given by her to Muḥammad, but the Prophet freed Zaid and thereafter treated him as an adopted son. Zaid may have had impressions of Christian teaching and discussed them with Muḥammad, but he became one of the first Muslims. There is a tradition that Muḥammad's first nurse was a Christian from Abyssinia, and later in life he received as concubine Māriyah the Copt from the ruler of Egypt. Khadīja had other Christian relatives; 'Uthmān b. al-Ḥuwayrith who aimed at being 'king' of Mecca about A.D. 605 had become a Christian with Byzantine help and was related to Khadīja's father. But all these are vague links, and it is unlikely that there was much Christian teaching imparted through them.

There seem to have been no Christian churches or regular teachers in Mecca or Medina. There would be traders and slaves whose knowledge of Christian doctrine would not be deep. But all round Arabia there were strong Christian kingdoms, with which Arab traders were in frequent contact. The Byzantine empire was Christian, of the Orthodox or Cyrillian teaching. Although the Persian empire was officially Zoroastrian, Christianity was strong, following the Nestorian or East Syrian teaching. An outpost of this church in Arabia was at al-Ḥīra and some of the Christian or Ḥanīf poets of Mecca may have been influenced from there. To the west were the Coptic churches of Egypt and Abyssinia, following Monophysite teaching.

But closer at hand, in the Yemen, was an organized Christian community, linked with Abyssinia which had occupied the Yemen in A.D. 525 and no doubt strengthened Christian life there. In San'ā' was a cathedral built by Abraha, who had ad-

[1] *The Life of Muhammad*, pp. 95f., 193.

vanced on Mecca with an elephant in his army in the year of Muḥammad's birth, and the site of this cathedral is still pointed out to visitors. It is said that Muḥammad once listened to a sermon by Quss, bishop of Najrān, at a festival near Mecca. From the Christian centre at Najrān visits were paid to Muḥammad on several occasions. Twenty Christians visited him in Mecca, either from Najrān or Abyssinia. It is said that when they heard the Qur'ān 'their eyes flowed with tears and they accepted God's call, believed in him, and declared his truth'. Then they went home.[1]

A deputation of sixty came from Najrān to Muḥammad at Medina. At the time of their prayers they stood and prayed in the mosque, the Prophet having said that they were to be allowed to do so. They prayed towards the east. There followed a long theological discussion. Finally, the Christians decided to hold to their religion, but they recognized Muḥammad as a prophet and left him in peace, asking for his help in settling disputes. 'Umar said, 'I never wanted an office more than I wanted that one and I hoped that I should get it'. But the Prophet appointed another mediator to Najrān.[2]

It is said that it was concerning these Christians of Najrān and Abyssinia that the Quranic words came that they were 'nearest in love' to Muslims. (5,85/82) And also the verses: 'Those to whom we have given the Book before it – they believe in it . . . When they hear vain talk they turn from it and say: "We have our works and ye have yours; peace be with you!" ' (28,52–55)

Later still when Muḥammad sent messengers from Medina to various kingdoms, he sent a particularly friendly message to the Negus of Abyssinia, speaking of their common faith. But the words of this, and the emperor's reply, in the later biographers, are not above dispute. Abyssinia of course had provided refuge for parties of emigrants from persecution as Muslims in Mecca before the Hijra, with the clear understanding that Christians would be the most friendly to Muslims. When the Negus died Muḥammad 'prayed over him and begged that his sins might be forgiven'.[3]

Christian monks in Arabia and Syria were regarded with

[1] *The Life of Muhammad*, pp. 14ff., 179. [2] *ibid.*, pp. 270ff. [3] *ibid.*, p. 155.

respect. There is the famous story of the monk Baḥīrā whose cell was at Buṣrā in Syria, 'who was well versed in the knowledge of Christians', and it is said that he had never stopped a passing caravan till one came by with the boy Muḥammad in it. After having insisted that the boy should leave the camels and join the others at the meal provided, it is said that Baḥīrā 'saw the seal of prophethood between his shoulders', and told his uncle that 'a great future lies before this nephew of yours'. Again, when he was travelling to Syria for Khadīja, Muḥammad stopped in the shade of a tree near a monk's cell and it is said that the latter exclaimed that 'none but a prophet ever sat beneath this tree'.[1]

These are not Quranic stories, but they show something of the sympathy between Muslims and monks in the early days. It is perhaps wandering ascetics who are praised in sura 9,113/112: 'Those who repent, those who serve, who give praise, who wander, who bow, who prostrate themselves, who urge to what is reputable, who refrain from what is disreputable.'

Not all monks were saints, but the origin of monasticism is recognized as being the desire to serve God. Yet the life of celibacy in enclosed communities is as foreign to the original spirit of Islam as it is to Judaism, or for that matter to early Christianity. The general Semitic attitude to life has been broadly described as 'world-affirming', as against the 'world-renouncing' spirit of India and the far east. The world is the creation of God, it was made 'very good', and man is to be 'fruitful, and multiply, and replenish the earth'. All things that are on the earth are given him for use. Therefore married life is the norm, for religious men as well as for others, and celibacy is foreign to the Bible and to the Qur'ān. The later Christian exaltation of virginity over marriage is a perversion that badly infected the church. Islam has never had a celibate priesthood; but neither have most Christian churches with the exception of Roman Catholicism.

In later Islam the growth of the Ṣūfī mystical movements was strongly influenced by the example of Christian monks. The very name Ṣūfī is said to come from *sūf*, the plain woollen robe

[1] *The Life of Muhammad*, pp. 79f., 82f.

of the Christian monk. Jesus was taken as the pattern of poverty and the ascetic life. But Muslim communities, like most Indian and Buddhist monasteries, were rarely enclosed, as were the great medieval monasteries of Europe. They were rather places of retreat to which men retired for a time, and which pious laymen could visit as well.

Christians and Muslims, when they were true to the spirit of their founders, were close to each other. Sūra 29,45/46 says: 'Dispute not with the People of the Book save in the fairer manner . . . and say, "We believe in what has been sent down to us, and what has been sent down to you; our God and your God is One." ' Yet they only occasionally united, and so their differences were regarded as means by which God tries them. If they rival each other in good works that is best, and God will eventually resolve their differences. 'Had God so willed, he would have made you one community, but (he hath not done so) in order that he might try you in regard to what has come to you; so strive to be foremost in what is good; it is to God that ye return, all of you, and he will announce to you that in which ye have been differing.' (5,53/48)

17

Conclusion

In his study of Jesus according to the Qur'ān Henri Michaud says: 'thus, after having tried to understand what the Qur'ān says about Jesus, we shall ask our brothers of Islam with very great anxiety: "Is this indeed what you believe about Jesus?" ' If there is a reply without ambiguity, he says, then an irenical dialogue can be begun.[1] This is assuming that the reply is favourable. But it may be negative. By isolating Jesus from the rest of the Qur'ān and the Islamic tradition one may arrive at a portrait of Jesus that is not the Jesus that Muslims know. There are several reasons for this and they must be considered briefly.

Jesus is mentioned in 15 sūras of the Qur'ān, but not in the other 99. 93 verses speak of him, but there are 6,226 (or 6,211) verses in the whole Qur'ān. He receives many honourable names but he is placed in the succession of the prophets, and teaching about the prophets is only one element in the Qur'ān.

The fundamental and all-pervading doctrine of the Qur'ān is the unity and transcendence of God. Parallels to this are rather in the Old Testament than the New, though they are assumed in the New Testament but modified by the concepts of grace and love. Association of other beings with God, and making images of him, are blasphemous. God is the supreme and only creator, and false 'gods have created nothing, but are themselves created' (25,3). All things belong to God, he is the

[1] *Jésus selon le Coran*, p. 10.

owner of all power and can do anything. Any power that man may have comes from God, who gives it to whom he wills and to whom all will return. In response to the divine gifts man should show gratitude, and to be ungrateful is *kufr* which came to mean unbelieving; the *kāfir* is ungrateful and unbelieving. In the Qur'ān, says Zaehner, you have 'as in no other book, the sense of an absolutely overwhelming Being proclaiming Himself to a people that had not known Him . . . Not even in the Old Testament do you have such an over-mastering insight into Omnipotence. Nowhere else is God revealed . . . as so utterly inscrutable, so tremendous, and so mysterious.'[1] Nevertheless, the nature of God is shown by the many attribute or 'beautiful names': 'the Merciful, the Compassionate' at the beginning of nearly every sura, and many terms throughout the suras: wise, powerful, oft-returning, bountiful, sublime, hearing, knowing, forgiving, etc.

The Qur'ān is 'the quintessence of prophecy', adds Zaehner. It is not a biography of Muḥammad, whose proper name occurs in it comparatively rarely (four times), though it is addressed to and through him and its message comes for many events in his life. But his own experience of the divine call and mission provides the link with other prophets and messengers. The prophets were sent to be obeyed, given a message and jurisdiction. The revelation given to the former prophets was reproduced in the latter, and 'the Book' brings guidance and light to 'the People of the Book'. These messages are the true 'signs' or evidence of the claims of the prophets, and they witness to the power of God in nature and his concern with human affairs. The prophetic messages agree, the one confirming the other; they appear to be repetition or confirmation, rather than development.

Much is said of the Last Things, of Judgement to come, and the short and early sūras in particular recall many of the eschatological teachings and symbolism of Jewish and Christian apocalyptic: Daniel, Revelation and apocryphal material. There are many sayings about the 'hour', the 'last day', or the 'day of resurrection', 'judgement' or 'distinction'. These show

[1] *At Sundry Times*, p. 27.

that the Qur'ān, like the Bible, teaches a linear view of history, its progression in a line, coming to a crisis, rather than going round in a circle in Indian fashion. Descriptions of Heaven and Hell, the 'Garden' and Gehennah (Jahannam), are closely reminiscent of other books. Men are judged according to belief or unbelief, yet moral actions are fundamental because belief in God and his way is the entrance to real goodness. A striking passage, probably referring to Jewish-Christian divisions, exalts conduct above dogma and recalls the parable of Judgement in Matthew 25: 'It is not by your dogmas, or the dogmas of the People of the Book . . . but whoever does works of righteousness, be it male or female, and is a believer – they will enter the Garden.' (4,122–123/123–124)

There is also a great deal of moral and legal matter in the Qur'ān, for it supplied to the pagan Arabs what Jews and Christians had received in the Bible. The duties or 'pillars' of Islam: prayer, almsgiving, fasting and pilgrimage, all follow on the major confession of God and his Prophet. Marriage and divorce, usury and gambling, food and drink, fighting and slavery, these and many other subjects are treated especially in those sūras which date from the larger community at Medina.[1]

Naturally then there is a great deal in the Qur'ān which does not refer to Jesus. In the New Testament he is the principal subject, but in the Qur'ān though prophet and Christ he comes along with others. It might be asked, however, whether Islam has paid enough attention to what is said about Jesus and whether later traditions have turned it away from the Gospel to which the Qur'ān refers.

Even so can Islam and Christianity be brought closer together? Michel Hayek, in his study of the Christ of Islam, writes of the similarities but also of the differences between the Church and the Mosque. There is not even the same *faith*, he says, for Christian faith implies the Cross as a new dimension, beyond the possibilities of natural intelligence. Abraham is the father of this faith, when as a figure of the eternal Father he offered his son. Islam, he says, rejects the Cross and hides behind

[1] R. Bell, *Introduction to the Qur'ān*, 1953, ch. VIII.

the adoration of the divine nature, the unfathomable mystery. Christianity, says Hayek, puts love as the starting place and the goal, whereas Islam rejects creative love and even more the communion of love with God.[1]

It is a pity that these provocative statements come at the beginning of what is otherwise an attractive and erudite work, for they are liable to offend Muslim readers and so defeat Hayek's professed purpose of rallying Christianity and Islam 'around the same notion of God . . . personal, creator, master of history and guide of salvation'.[2] There is no doubt that Christians hold firmly to the Cross as a historical fact, but they are not bound to accept theories that would interpret it in terms of legal satisfaction or sacrificial substitution. Christians also hold strongly to belief in the love of God, but so have many Muslim Ṣūfīs and they sought justification in those words of the Qur'ān which spoke of God as 'compassionate, loving' (11,92/90; 85,14) and nearer to man than his jugular vein. (50,15/16)

Basic both to Christianity and Islam is belief in one God and his religious and moral guidance of men. Christians have this partly in the Old Testament, which has always been an indispensable background for further Christian thinking. The Arabs had no such background; it was given to them in the Qur'ān, and this is the reason for its many social and practical teachings.

Developing from the Old Testament, the New Testament came to give higher and more refined teachings, leaving aside some of the barbaric notions of earlier passages. Jesus taught: 'Love your enemies, and pray for them that persecute you.' (Matt. 5,44) And Jesus not only said this but practised it in his life, even at the cross. This led to the particular interpretation which was given to Christ, as revelation and Word of God. In other traditions the word of God may come to man, as a spoken directive or a written law. In the New Testament the Gospel, the Good News of Jesus, is not only a message or a written word, but it is inextricably bound up with a person. The importance of Jesus is not only in his moral maxims, such as the Sermon on the Mount, which even an agnostic might try to follow. But

[1] *Le Christ de l'Islam*, p. 25. [2] *ibid.*, p. 26.

Jesus is seen as Christ in himself, his life, healings, death and resurrection. These are the 'evidences' with which Christ came, his person in addition to his teachings, and they give new light on the nature of God. It was not because of the words of Jesus only, but through his life and death, that Christians came to say 'God is love'. In fact it is curious that this phrase 'God is love', which is held to typify Christian faith, does not occur in the Gospels but in the epistles which are a reflection on the difference that Christ had made to the understanding of God. (1 John 4,8) This is why the Gospels cannot really be isolated from the rest of the New Testament. For however imperfectly his followers understood him, or however haltingly they expressed their faith, they were trying to say what Christ had meant to them and could mean to the world. The Gospels are four, not one, because they attempt to show how Christ appeared to his many followers; Good News not only in speech but in action.

Such a view of Christ may be hard for a Muslim to accept, but it is at least worth the effort at making it understandable. And in modern times a great deal of rethinking of traditional doctrines and their expression is being done, so that dialogue between the religions is much easier than for centuries past. Some doctrines, at least, have been expressed in language that is out-dated and often incomprehensible. Whatever the term 'Son of God' may have meant originally to Jews and Gentiles, it is liable to misunderstanding today, not only to Muslims but also to many Christians. Modern debates over the symbolism or 'mythology' of Christian theology are evidence of the need for fresh and meaningful language about the significance of Christ. Ideas that Christ came from 'up there', 'intervened' in the world, and played a super-human role, may need changing to fit conceptions of God as ever-present in the world and of Jesus as fully human and historical. Islam may share with Christianity in this process of rethinking.

It is sometimes said that Islam has been blind to Christ, neglectful of what the Qur'ān itself says, and ignorant of the Gospel to which the Qur'ān refers. But Christianity also has often been blind to Christ, Docetic in its view of his humanity, and impervious to the prophetic correction that Islam maintained to some dogmas. The divisions of Christians were a scandal from the early days. 'The sects differed among themselves', says the Qur'ān continually and sadly. A later Arab historian remarked acidly, 'where ten Christians met they formed eleven different opinions'. Why should this be? Clearly many differences arose in the early centuries, when this Semitic faith was expressed through a Greek medium. It would be easy to attribute it all to the apostle Paul, but he was himself a Hebrew, and supported by other New Testament Jewish writers. Yet perhaps those early feelings after the expression of Christian faith in a wider environment need not have been fixed so rigidly. The search for uniformity led to heresy and division, and there has never been complete unity.

When the newly discovered Gnostic apocryphal writings, such as the so-called Gospel of Thomas, are examined, one may feel thankful that orthodox Christianity rejected the extremes of Neo-Platonic mysticism. But did the church keep close enough to its Biblical roots? Early Islam, thanks to its Semitic background and original isolation, was even more free from Greek speculation. Its prophetic witness to the unity of God, and in general to the humanity of Jesus and his mother, was a needful corrective which the church largely ignored. In the rethinking of doctrinal expression today Islam and Christianity can learn much from each other. Both need to look back to 'the rock whence ye were hewn, and to the hole of the pit whence ye were digged'. (Isaiah 51,1)

But how shall they learn if they do not read each other's scriptures? Until modern times, and still very widely, it has been true that most Muslims and Christians have been ignorant of each other's sacred books. 'To the average Muslim, for communal reasons which have no proper right to place it, there is a wide ban on the Gospel. Deep and significant implications of the Qur'ān are unknown to the average Christian . . . It is not only the damage this does which should appal us, but the fact that most people in both communities are quite content to have it so. Indeed, they take a complacent pride that it is entirely right and creditable. The Qur'ān is thus a closed book to Christians because the Muslim community "possesses" it.

Christian faith is a closed realm to the Muslim because it is the faith of Christians.'[1]

Many of the early Muslim writers had studied and appreciated the Bible, Old and New Testaments. Ṭabarī in particular quoted the Bible frequently and regarded it as inspired. But later centuries widened the gap between the religions and their scriptures. Crusades and Holy Wars, Inquisitions and persecutions, alienated those who should have been 'nearest in love' to one another. Happily there are many clear signs now that times and feelings are changing. The growing unity of the world, the spread of literature and the use of translations, personal and spiritual contacts, help to overcome political and religious imperialism. Many Muslims now read the Bible, and there are many translations of the Qur'ān in European languages. Evidence of this is seen in a number of lives of Jesus written by Muslims. These have appeared in several Islamic countries, and particularly in Egypt where 'Abd Al-Ḥamīd Al-Saḥḥār published *The Messiah, Jesus son of Mary* in 1952, 'Abbās Maḥmūd Al-'Aqqād brought out *The Genius of Christ* in 1952, Khālid M. Khālid's book *Together on the Road, Muhammad and Jesus* appeared in 1958, and Dr Kāmel Hussein's *City of Wrong, A Friday in Jerusalem*, was published in 1954 and was awarded the State Prize for Literature in Cairo in 1957.

Reading the Bible has given Muslim writers much fuller knowledge of the life of Jesus. But how far has this brought an understanding of his significance for religion and personal experience? In days gone by most Muslims were content to think of Jesus, even though respectfully, as one of the prophets. So his life might be interesting, historically, like the lives of other prophets of the Hebrew tradition. But the Qur'ān itself, we have seen, does not only or even most commonly call Jesus a prophet. He is called Messiah eleven times, and many other titles are bestowed upon him. In the Bible John the Baptist was said to be 'more than a prophet', and in the Qur'ān Jesus is much more. In the Bible, too, the importance of Jesus even in the early days in Galilee is more than prophetical exhortation or moral guidance. His Gospel is both his word and his person.

[1] K. Cragg, *The Dome and the Rock*, 1964, p. 219.

In Islam there is clearly a mystery about Jesus. It was accepted generally that his birth was unusual, comparable only with that of Adam. On the common interpretation of sūra 4,156/157 Jesus would be the only man in history who had not died. But if it felt after the mystery this interpretation did not grasp it. The stark tragedy of the crucifixion reveals depths of the human and divine natures that remain unapprehended. Yet the challenge remains, to search for the truth of the revelation of love and the relationship of God to man which appeared in the person of Christ. 'What think ye of Christ?' is still a question to be answered.

To the Christian also there is a challenge. It is too easily assumed that all traditional doctrines are firmly based on the Bible. The Semitic view of God may need to be cleared of some Greek theories that have overlaid it. Then if theology is to make contact with the modern world it must express itself in a meaningful way. Terms like Son of God, Trinity and Salvation need to be re-shaped and given new point. Concepts of prophecy, inspiration and revelation must be re-examined in view of the undoubted revelation of God in Muḥammad and in the Qur'ān. Then much more real charity and generous understanding must be shown to members of other faiths. The example of Islam towards other People of the Book often puts us to shame. Christians always need to remember the words of Jesus, 'Why call me, Lord, Lord, and do not the things which I say?'

It is to encourage study, self-examination, dialogue and searching the scriptures that this book has been written. Much wider acquaintance with the holy books is one of the most useful first steps to take. Let more Christians read the Qur'ān and more Muslims study the Bible, so as to extend understanding and reconciliation. For those who would discover the significance of Jesus in the Qur'ān a knowledge of the Gospel is essential. Jesus was not simply a figure of the past, of only local Jewish significance, but a universality emerges in the Gospel that is suggested in the Qur'ān. The Qur'ān calls Jesus 'a sign to all beings' (21,91), his family was chosen 'above the worlds' (3,30/33), and he himself was sent 'in order that we may make him a sign unto men'. (19,21) Yet the Qur'ān does not claim to give all the teachings of Jesus, nor does it set out to recount the whole story of his life and compassion, his healings and his death. These are in the Gospel, to which the Qur'ān refers, which it confirms, and over which it claims to act as protector against outside detractors and internal divisions.

General Index

Aaron, sister of, 64, 78
'abd, see Servant
'Abd al-Tafāhum, 89f., 106ff., 112ff., 121
Abraham, 19f., 39, 40, 43, 64, 103, 150, 154f., 168
abrogation, 121
Abū Bakr, 31
Abū Jahl, 23
Abyssinia, see Ethiopia
Adam, 31, 40, 43, 46, 49, 52, 64, 69f., 81, 103, 172
Adoptionism, 80, 119, 127ff., 137
Advent, see Second Coming
Affair, command, amr, 51, 139
Aḥmad Khān, 70, 85, 113, 130, 147
Aḥmadiyya, 32, 112, 113
aḥmadu, 96ff.
'Alī b. Abī Ṭālib, 23
'Alī, M., 22, 32n., 35, 50, 70, 71, 85f., 88, 113
'Alī, Y., 50, 76, 79, 107, 148
Allāh, use of divine name, 13
alms, zakāt, 57, 76
Altaner, B., 27n., 28, 48
amr, see Affair
Ananikian, M. H., 147n.
Anawati, G. C., 115
Andrae, T., 111
angels, 30, 34, 67, 70, 109; and see Gabriel
Annunciation, 16, 53f., Ch. 7
anṣār, see Helpers
Anti-Christ, 124
Antidicomarianites, 135
Apocrypha, 26ff., 42, 48, 55, 64, 65, 76f., 81, 86, 104, 109, 127, 147
Apostle, see Messenger
Apostles, ḥawārīyūn, 26, 44, 93, 153
al-'Aqqād, 'Abbās, 33, 172
Arabic Infancy Gospel, 27ff., 77f., 84
Arabic New Testament, 17f., 146, 161
Arabic Qur'ān, 38, 145
Arberry, A. J., 13, 30, 38, 46, 52, 53, 109
Ascension, exaltation, 16, 53, Ch. 12
āya, see Sign
Āzād, Maulana, 68, 70, 88
al-Azraqī, 66

Baḥīrā, 164
al-Baiḍāwī, 12, 17, 22, 31, 45, 53, 55, 60, 64, 65, 69, 70, 78, 85, 87, 93f., 105f., 111, 122f., 124, 161

Quranic Index

Verses on the left from Fluegel, on the right from the Cairo edition

Biblical Index